A Student's Guide
To Saint-Exupéry

STUDENT GUIDES TO EUROPEAN
LITERATURE

General Editor: Brian Masters
Molière, by Brian Masters
Sartre, by Brian Masters
Goethe, by F. J. Lamport
Rabelais, by Brian Masters
Corneille, by J. H. Broome
Böll, by Enid Macpherson
Kafka, by Anthony Thorlby
Saint-Exupéry, by Brian Masters

A Student's Guide To Saint-Exupéry

by

BRIAN MASTERS

HEINEMANN EDUCATIONAL
BOOKS LTD   LONDON

Heinemann Educational Books Ltd
LONDON EDINBURGH MELBOURNE SINGAPORE
NEW DELHI TORONTO AUCKLAND
JOHANNESBURG HONG KONG
NAIROBI IBADAN KUALA LUMPUR

ISBN 0 435 37579 2

Published by
Heinemann Educational Books Ltd
48 Charles Street, London W1X 8AH
Printed in Great Britain by
Richard Clay (The Chaucer Press) Ltd
Bungay, Suffolk

Contents

to Alistair

Foreword and Acknowledgements

This book is intended to summarize the major themes of Saint-Exupéry's work, which it is hoped will be of assistance to students approaching the author for the first time.

For purposes of organization, a separate chapter has been devoted to each of the principal works. However, the student is advised not to adhere strictly to this system. Saint-Exupéry returned to the same themes again and again, and consequently there is much, in *Pilote de Guerre* for example, which is relevant to an understanding of *Terre des Hommes*, and vice versa.

It has been assumed that students will use the scholastic editions of Saint-Exupéry's works, where available, and page references to *Vol de Nuit*, *Terre des Hommes*, and *Le Petit Prince* therefore apply to the editions published by Heinemann Educational Books Ltd. All other works quoted are referred to in their original Gallimard editions, with the exception of *Citadelle*, for which the Gallimard Pléiade edition has been used.

The author wishes to thank Messrs Gallimard for their kind permission to quote from the works of Saint-Exupéry of which they control the copyright.

A suggested list of books for further study is included at the end.

Old Head, Co. Mayo, Ireland, 1971

La grandeur, en effet, de ma civilisation, c'est que cent mineurs s'y doivent de risquer leur vie pour le sauvetage d'un seul mineur enseveli. Ils sauvent l'Homme.

1

Biographical Introduction

Antoine-Jean-Baptiste-Marie-Roger de Saint-Exupéry, son and heir of the Count Jean-Marie de Saint-Exupéry and of Marie Boyer de Fonscolombe, was born at a house in Lyon on 29 June 1900. Of noble stock on both sides, Antoine was to be the last male in a family of ancient lineage dating back to the fourth century.

There were two elder sisters, Marie-Magdaleine and Simone, and Antoine was followed by a brother, François, and another sister, Gabrielle. In 1904 the Count died, leaving the Countess to raise five small children. The family was not by any means wealthy.

Antoine's childhood was henceforth divided between two castles; the summer was spent at the property of an aunt, Saint-Maurice-de-Remens (Ain), and the winter with the maternal grandmother at the Château-de-la-Mole (Var). Antoine's biographers are agreed that his early years were luminously happy. His time was spent exploring deserted houses, taming tortoises or white rats, or, and this most interestingly, writing poetry and playing with mechanical objects. Thus the two poles of his life had begun to exert their influence by the age of eight. On the one hand, Antoine would read his verses to his patient mother at all hours of the night; on the other hand, his insatiable passion for technical problems led him to invent and construct a bicycle with wings.

The family took up residence at Le Mans in 1909, and Antoine transferred to the Jesuit College of Notre-Dame de Sainte-Croix. His school-work was honourable, but not spectacular.

He attempted to translate Julius Caesar in secret, in the hope of discovering how the Roman men-of-war worked.

At the age of twelve, an event of singular importance occurred. At the nearby aerodrome of Ambérieu, Antoine watched with fascination as the pilot Védrines took his aircraft on a demonstration flight. Using the charm which he was later to exert on all he met, the little boy persuaded the famous airman to take him up for a spin. The die was cast.

Significantly, Antoine's first extant verses, inspired no doubt by this experience, date from the same year. Only three lines remain, but they are enough to indicate an extraordinary sensitivity in a boy of twelve:

Les ailes frémissaient sous le souffle du soir
Le moteur de son chant berçait l'âme endormie
Le soleil nous frôlait de sa couleur pâlie.

In 1914, the family left Le Mans. Antoine and François spent one unhappy term at a school in Villefranche, and then transferred to a school in Switzerland. Mme de Saint-Exupéry became a nurse at the hospital of Ambérieu.

The two boys hurried back to France in 1917, when François' health began to give cause for anxiety. The boy died in July of that year of cardiac rheumatism, at the age of fifteen. Antoine was at his deathbed. The two brothers had been extremely close, and the sudden death was a grave shock to Antoine, who was himself barely seventeen years old. His young brother's last words were a plea to their mother not to worry on his account, for he would be much happier where he was going than had he lived to suffer in this world.

That same year, Antoine passed his school examinations, and went to the École Bossuet in Paris, to prepare for entrance to naval college. Unfortunately, although his performance in mathematics was astonishing, he received such a poor mark in French composition, and failed so miserably in the orals, that his application was refused.

Antoine became for a while an unenthusiastic student of

architecture, living in a cheap hotel in Paris, until his military service took him to Strasbourg, where he was attached to a flying regiment and assigned to the repair shed. But Antoine wanted to fly. By scrupulously saving pennies from his meagre grant, he was able to pay for flying lessons at the base. After only one and a half hours' instruction, he flew solo (without permission), and was miraculously able to land. He was now twenty-one years old.

The following year, his pilot's licence in his pocket, Antoine de Saint-Exupéry was appointed a military pilot. In 1923 he was demobilized, and returned to Paris.

The earthbound life of Paris was no longer able to satisfy him. He yearned to join the Air Force. At the same time, he became engaged to Louise de Vilmorin, whose family objected to their daughter's fiancé being a pilot. Flying was still a novel and dangerous profession in 1923, without the *cachet* of respectability that it now has. So Saint-Exupéry renounced his ambition for the time being, and took a job as travelling-salesman for Saurer lorries. It was not a happy choice. In eighteen months, he succeeded in selling but one lorry; meanwhile, he was writing a great deal, and destroying as much.

1926 is a capital year. His first published work, a short story called *L'aviateur*, appeared in the revue *Le Navire d'Argent*. He left the Saurer company, and took a position as flying instructor. Meantime, his engagement had been broken off. Like the hero of *Courrier Sud*, Saint-Exupéry had failed in love, and was to take refuge in a life of action. In November of that year, with the help of one of his old teachers, he was introduced to Didier Daurat, the pioneer pilot and director of the mail-flights from Toulouse to Dakar, operated by the Latécoère company. Daurat offered him an administrative post with the company, but he refused, stating quite frankly his desire to fly. Daurat deferred to the young man's enthusiasm.

Didier Daurat was to be the major influence on Saint-Exupéry's life and work. A man with a vision, and an iron determination to see that vision realized, Daurat inspired his pilots with a loyalty without which, in these pioneer days of civil aviation, the achievements of *La Ligne* might never have occurred. Among the pilots under his command were two who have taken their place in the history of aviation, and were to be immortalized in the books of Saint-Exupéry – Jean Mermoz and Henri Guillaumet.

One of the difficulties which threatened the success of the Line was the hostility of the Moors over whose territory the pilots had to fly on their route from Casablanca to Dakar, coupled with the obstinate non-co-operation of the Spanish government. In 1927, Daurat appointed Saint-Exupéry chief of the air-station at Cap Juby on the African coast. It is a tribute to Saint-Exupéry's diplomacy and charm that, during his eighteen months at Cap Juby, he not only established cordial relations with the Spanish authorities, but won the undying friendship of the dangerous and dissident Moors.

His sojourn at Cap Juby was by no means entirely absorbed in administrative or diplomatic duties. Frequent were the crashes or disappearance of pilots in the desert, and Saint-Exupéry was constantly flying in search of lost airmen. It was also at Cap Juby, hundreds of miles from any centre of civilized life, bounded on one side by the Atlantic, and on three sides by the desert, that he wrote his first book.

The manuscript of *Courrier Sud* was delivered to Gallimard in Paris in 1929, and published the following year. In October of 1929, Saint-Exupéry was invited to join Daurat, Guillaumet, and Mermoz in South America, where the Latécoère company were establishing routes over unknown territory. Saint-Exupéry, appointed director of the Argentinian route, himself carried out reconnaissance flights, established bases, and founded the Patagonian route from Buenos Aires to Tierra del Fuego which is used today. Daurat's main ambition at this time was to initiate night-flying, which, in the days when runways were not illuminated, was unheard of. In this he succeeded, and incidentally gave Saint-Exupéry the subject for his next book, *Vol de Nuit*.

In 1930, Saint-Exupéry was decorated with the Legion of Honour for his services to aviation. At the end of that year, he met the beautiful and vivacious young widow Consuelo Suncin, proposed marriage, and arranged the wedding in France three months later.

The marriage was to prove somewhat erratic, affording Saint-Exupéry happiness and worry in equal measure. Consuelo enjoyed society gatherings, parties, city life, and minks; Saint-Exupéry was more at ease with one friend than a host of strangers, and preferred rough country living to the grandest hotel suite. Their separate tastes led to occasional friction, and to periods when they saw little of each other. But their life together was, on the whole, colourful and exciting.

Vol de Nuit was published in 1931, and awarded the coveted Prix Fémina. Less happily, as the result of a sordid financial scandal, the Latécoère company was taken over and absorbed into the new Air France. The heroic pioneer days were at an end.

There followed a protracted period of extreme unhappiness for Saint-Exupéry. In spite of the royalties from *Vol de Nuit*, he was troubled with persistent penury. He had no job, and no prospect of employment. The liberating excitement had gone out of his life with the downfall of the South American company. He was once more earthbound, never a happy condition for him. And, worst of all, his literary success gave rise to bitter jealousy. He was accused of being an amateur pilot who only joined the company of real men like Mermoz in order to exploit them for literary gain. No accusation could have been more cruelly unfair. The depth of his suffering at this time is attested by a letter he wrote to Guillaumet:

> Guillaumet, il paraît que tu arrives, et j'en ai le coeur un peu battant. Si tu savais quelle terrible vie j'ai menée depuis ton départ, et quel immense dégoût de la vie j'ai peu à peu appris à ressentir. Parce que j'avais écrit ce malheureux livre, j'ai été condamné à la misère et à l'inimitié de mes camarades. Mermoz te dira quelle réputation ceux qui ne m'ont pas vu et que j'aimais tant

> m'ont peu à peu faite. On te dira combien je suis préten-
> tieux! Et pas un, de Toulouse à Dakar, qui en doute. Un
> de mes plus graves soucies a été aussi ma dette, mais je
> n'ai même pas toujours pu payer mon gaz et je vis sur mes
> vieux vêtements d'il y a trois ans. . . .
> . . . Ne va pas à l'hôtel. Installe-toi dans mon appartement,
> il est à toi. Moi, je vais travailler à la campagne dans
> quatre ou cinq jours. Tu seras comme chez toi et tu auras
> le téléphone, ce qui est plus commode. Mais peut-être
> refuseras-tu! Et peut-être faudra-t-il m'avouer que j'ai
> perdu même la meilleure de mes amitiés.

Any reader of Saint-Exupéry's books will know what importance he attached to comradeship, and will appreciate the hurt
which his detractors caused him. Happily, Guillaumet did
not join them.

The remainder of the thirties was a period of near-stagnation.
He was sent by *Paris-Soir* to Moscow and to Madrid as a
reporter, and went on his own account to Berlin to observe
nazism at close quarters. The only spark of real interest was
occasioned by his sudden decision, at the end of 1935, to com-
pete for the prize offered to anyone who could beat the established flying record from Paris to Saigon. The venture was ill-
fated. After four hours' flight, he crashed in the Libyan desert,
and he and his mechanic Prévot all but died of thirst for three
days before they were rescued. It was not the first, nor was it
to be the last time that Saint-Exupéry flirted with death. (In
1933, he crashed in the Mediterranean and almost drowned;
in 1938, he crashed in Guatemala, permanently crippling a
shoulder, and only resisting the amputation of an arm by sheer
obstinacy.)

André Gide, who had written an eulogistic preface to *Vol de
Nuit* and was a fervent admirer of Saint-Exupéry's literary
talent, suggested the format of his next book, *Terre des Hommes*, which he wrote during 1938. Published in 1939, the book
won the Grand Prix du Roman awarded by the Académie
Française. Saint-Exupéry was now a celebrated author on both
sides of the Atlantic.

With the outbreak of the Second World War, he overcame objections to his fitness, and joined the reconnaissance group 2/33 as a pilot. His flight over Arras was to inspire his next work *Pilote de Guerre* (called, in translation, *Flight to Arras*). After the French defeat, the group was transferred to Algiers, and Saint-Exupéry demobolized. He stayed with his sister for a while at Agay, writing his posthumous *Citadelle*, and at the end of 1940, embarked for the United States. In November, his adored friend Guillaumet was shot down. Mermoz had disappeared in the Atlantic in 1936.

The French colony in New York was bitterly divided. Saint-Exupéry refused to join any of the factions, calling instead for the reconciliation of all Frenchmen. His coldness towards the Gaullists won him the unquenchable enmity of the General, whose dismissive hostility was to cause him much pain in the last years.

Flight to Arras was published in New York in 1942, and had a remarkable immediate impact. Its author was hailed as the free world's spokesman against Hitler's *Mein Kampf*. Though banned in France by the Vichy government, the book was America's premier best-seller for six months. The following year, *Lettre à Un Otage* and *Le Petit Prince* both appeared. But Saint-Exupéry was impatient to return to combat.

By virtue of pulling a number of strings, he was allowed to join the 2/33 group in North Africa. But not for long. The Americans, pointing out that the age limit for combat pilots was thirty-five years, secured his dismissal.

Enforced inactivity was accompanied by gathering neurosis. Saint-Exupéry resumed work on *Citadelle*, but he was morose and unhappy, a prey to hypochondria and melancholy. For eight months he remained in Algiers, a constant burden to his friend Dr Pellissier, disillusioned and embittered by the continued bickerings of his countrymen. More than anything else, it was the refusal of the authorities to allow him to contribute to the fight in an active capacity which induced his debilitating sense of gnawing frustration. Richard Rumbold and Margaret

Stewart (who were both flyers and thereby better able to understand him than most), have written of this period:

> It is difficult, perhaps, for anyone but an airman to realize all the implications of being grounded. Stripped of his wings, pinioned to earth, the airman feels a sense of loss and deprivation, almost like a symbolical shearing. For the air has become a part of himself and his life; it is bound up with his freedom, his feeling of power, his ability to aspire towards the pinnacles and the heights.
>
> *(The Winged Life*, pp. 201–10)

The gravity of such deprivation was to Saint-Exupéry equivalent to a figurative castration of his powers. As he himself wrote, 'j'ai besoin, pour être, de participer'.

More strings were pulled, as a result of which he persuaded General Eakers to give special permission, in spite of his forty-three years, for further reconnaissance flights. The condition was that his missions should be limited to five.

It was useless to attempt to clip Saint-Exupéry's wings. After the seventh mission, his superiors decided that he should be let into the secret of the impending American offensive, thereby protecting him against himself, since nobody who knew of the plan was allowed, for security reasons, to take part in missions. Saint-Exupéry was becoming increasingly careless and absent-minded; anxiety was felt for his safety.

It was arranged that he should be told on 1 August 1944. On 31 July, he took off on his eighth mission, at 8.30 a.m., with reserves of fuel for six hours. By 2.30 p.m., he had not returned. That evening, he was declared lost.

It is not known whether Antoine de Saint-Exupéry crashed on land or sea, whether as the result of an accident or an attack by a German aircraft. No trace of his aeroplane was ever found.

*   *   *   *   *

Saint-Exupéry was, by all accounts, a remarkable man. The whole of France was stunned by his death. His friends vied with each other in their praise of his qualities – his probity, integrity, fidelity had no equal. There seems to have been not one man who ever met him and was not captivated by his honest charm. Léon Werth wrote that he was, in many instances, greater than his legend. Léon-Paul Fargue wrote the most moving obituary:

> C'était toujours un événement que de lui serrer la main.
> . . . Tout simplement, il était charmant, et il avait, au fond de son coeur honnête et généreux, de la bienveillance, de la compréhension et de la gentillesse pour tout le monde.
> . . . C'était un bon grand diable de loyauté, de soulagement et de foi que nous ne pouvons nous consoler d'avoir perdu. . . . Je l'ai beaucoup aimé, et je le pleurerai toujours.
>
> (*Confluences*, Nos. 12–14, 1947)

Although he wrote that mere courage did not impress him, he was a naturally courageous man. Readers of any of his biographies will be acquainted with the words of Henri Guillaumet who, when lost in the Andes, saw but was not seen by an aircraft looking for him. 'I knew it was Saint-Ex, for no one else would have dared fly so low.'

He was not a great pilot, in the manner of Mermoz; he was too clumsy and absent-minded to have the necessary qualities for concentration. Many are the stories of his taking off without closing the cockpit, or of reading a book while he should be thinking of landing. Some at least of his numerous accidents were directly attributable to carelessness.

He had a total disregard for material comfort. His various lodgings were always in a mess, his shirts had sometimes to be held together with pins. He was, as Renée de Saussine has said, 'not of this world'.

His ever-curious mind was capable of encyclopedic activity. His notebook testifies the scope of his interest – politics, physics, mathematics, economics, sociology; he was in many ways typical of the Renaissance Universal Man, who coupled action with intellectual energy in equal measure. A professor of mathematics has said that Saint-Exupéry might have been one of the great mathematicians of his generation. He was a tireless inventor, designing, among a score of other things, a precision-finding instrument on the radar principle, and evolving a theory of mass based on electro-magnetic waves.

Add to this that he was possessed of the most astonishing psychic powers, and one begins to understand the enthusiasm of those who knew him and hailed him as a universal genius.

In spite of his charm, Saint-Exupéry was not a man to indulge in cosy confidences. Perhaps it was his profound humility that prevented him from opening his heart too frequently. It is a pity, for we only have the barest indications of his personal religious position, which is so important to an understanding of his work. It seems that he lost his faith before he was twenty. He admitted to one friend that, had he been truly religious, he might have been a monk. But it is evident from his writing, and his emphasis on the 'divinity' within men, that he remained an anguished idealist searching for a focus for his latent religious fervour. The focus was provided eventually by his Humanism.

Saint-Exupéry is almost unique in having dedicated his whole life to the values in which he believed. Hypocrisy was totally alien to his nature. Not content to counsel, he gave an example. He never recommended anything which he had not first proven to be possible by his own experience. Writing books was not his principal interest; the greater part of his energy was devoted to living. As Pierre de Boisdeffre has written, he was 'un homme véritable, et non un homme de papier'. And Max-Pol Fouchet: 'Un vivant magnifique, non pas un homme de plume, mais un homme de vie.'

Not that his literary efforts were dilettante. He attached great importance to his writing, which he wanted to be taken as seriously as he himself took life. In a letter to his mother, he wrote:

> Il faut me chercher tel que je suis dans ce que j'écris et qui est le résultat scrupuleux et réfléchi de ce que je pense et vois.

Just how scrupulous was his writing is attested by the story of an American friend who was given nearly a hundred versions of the same page to read and comment upon. *Vol de Nuit* was four times its present length before Saint-Exupéry edited it.

And what of his literary value?

Until quite recently, the works of Saint-Exupéry were universally admired both for their ennobling, moral influence, and for the purity of their style. Nowadays, it is more common to question their value. Two critics in particular, who must be considered if only for the attention which they have been given, have launched highly vituperative, even petulant, attacks. Jean Cau is of the opinion that Saint-Exupéry has:

> une pensée d'une faiblesse insigne et d'une profondeur telle que l'eau vous en arrive aux chevilles . . . je conseille de mettre Saint-Exupéry (on ne m'a d'ailleurs pas attendu pour le faire) entre les mains des adolescents de quatorze ans.

While his colleague, J.-F. Revel, is yet more insulting:

> une ânerie verbeuse devient profonde vérité philosophique si on la fait décoller du sol pour l'élever à sept mille pieds de haut. Le crétinisme sous cockpit prend des allures de sagesse.

Other, less vindictive, critics have discerned in Saint-Exupéry's work a dangerous tendency towards pontification.

If the public is any judge (and who dares to suggest that it is not?), then Saint-Exupéry need fear nothing from his critics. For he has sold more copies of his books than any other French writer of the twentieth century. Perhaps the public feels, with Léon Werth, that Antoine de Saint-Exupéry was 'le seul écrivain de notre temps que la gloire toucha'.

2

Courrier Sud

Written during the period at Cap Juby, and published in 1929 before his departure to Argentina, Saint-Exupéry's first novel is the story of a man's search for a deeper significance to life than that afforded by material security or emotional comfort. In this book, Saint-Exupéry poses questions to which his later work was to find the answers.

Jacques Bernis is a pilot carrying mail between Toulouse and Dakar. His solitary and nomadic existence, while seeming to lend a purpose to his life, robs him of the normal pleasures of a permanent relationship with any one person or a lasting sense of belonging to any one place. He lives in a succession of hotel rooms, between flights, all of which are empty of any personal meaning. He is permanently unattached and 'free', yet sometimes yearns, in the loneliness of his cockpit, to throw down roots, to belong, to surround himself with reassuring recognizable possessions.

Passing through Paris, he seeks out a childhood friend, Geneviève, whom he finds married, in the apparent stability of a home. The walls and objects which surround her, and which are dear to her, provide the kind of support and protection which Bernis' wandering existence lacks. Her life seems ordered and peaceful in her own little kingdom.

But the edifice crumbles when her child dies. Her husband, Herlin, wallows in self-pity, and cruelly makes her suffer in order that he may still retain the power of love over her. The security of her identity with possessions now offers little succour in face of the appalling injustice of death. Having first sought refuge in the continued order of her existence, she then turns to Bernis, and they decide to flee together and start life anew.

Two days later, after trivial irritations which dull their sense of rebirth (the car breaks down in the rain, hotels are closed, etc.), Bernis realizes that Geneviève is limbless without the belongings which gave a décor to her life and which alone can cushion her. She is too closely tied to them for adventure and rebirth to be any longer possible. She returns to Paris, and Bernis is once more alone and uprooted.

He turns briefly to religion, but is disgusted with its irrelevance to life. Passionate love with a stranger affords only momentary pleasure and is meaningless in the long term. Only the vocation and its responsibilities remain. After a final visit to Geneviève, which confirms the unbridgeable gulf which separates their two kinds of existence, and the impossibility of their ever understanding each other, Bernis returns to Toulouse and to flying. Flying will at least provide an escape from the staggering mediocrity of daily life, a contact with nature and the stars; they are his permanence. His final contact with human life is a meeting with an old man in the desert, when his aircraft breaks down. The following day, he crashes and is killed. The mail flights will continue.

A. Security

Saint-Exupéry recognizes the powerful stabilizing influence of a home and possessions which, in their solidity and permanence, offer a challenge to the transience of human life.

1. Ces coutumes, ces conventions, ces lois, tout ce dont tu ne sens pas la nécessité, tout ce dont tu t'es évadé . . . C'est cela qui lui donne un cadre. Il faut, autour de soi, pour exister, des réalités qui durent.
   (*Courrier Sud*, pp. 95–6)
2. Elle aime, de la paume, caresser la pierre, caresser ce qu'il y a dans la maison de plus sûr et de plus durable. Ce qui peut vous porter longtemps comme un navire . .
   (ibid., p. 100)

3. Elle revoit cette maison à travers les tilleuls épais. C'est ce qu'il y avait de plus stable qui arrivait à la surface: ce perron de pierre larges qui se continuait dans la terre.

(ibid., p. 103)

Bernis envies this sureness of Geneviève in her home, the obscure, binding relationship which she has with things around her. She is 'sûre d'elle-même et liée à tout et faisant partie d'un grand concert'. (p. 76) On her return to Paris, her first thought is to re-establish the order in her home which is her necessary support:

4. Les draps froids et défaits, des serviettes jetées sur les meubles, une chaise tombée. Il faut qu'elle s'oppose en hâte à cette débâcle des choses. Il faut tirer en hâte ce fauteuil à sa place, ce vase, ce livre. Il faut qu'elle s'épuise vainement à refaire l'attitude des choses qui entourent la vie.   (ibid., p. 90)

Whenever Bernis lands, he finds his friends unchanged, continuing the life which they passively led when he last flew away from them. He talks of their being embarked on a ship, whose destination they know. They are aware of their future, for it will be the same as their past. He comes to realize that the cost of this apparent security is a docile abnegation of life, and that he is wrong to envy Geneviève. Security is a trap, which takes hold of one like a vice, and from which it is difficult to escape. It is the very denial of life, the acceptance of permanent and voluntary imprisonment:

5. Ce monde, nous le retrouvions chaque fois, comme les matelots bretons retrouvent leur village de carte postale et leur fiancée trop fidèle, à leur retour à peine vieillie. Toujours pareille, la gravure d'un livre d'enfance. A reconnaître tout si bien en place, si bien réglé par le destin, nous avions peur de quelquechose d'obscur. Bernis s'informait d'un ami: 'Mais oui. Le même. Ses affaires ne vont pas bien fort. Enfin, tu sais . . . la vie.' Tous étaient prisonniers d'eux-mêmes, limités par ce frein obscur et non comme lui, ce fugitif, cet enfant pauvre, ce magicien.   (ibid., p. 49)

The danger is that one's life, subordinate to order and security, may be submerged in trivia:

> 6. Nous nous sentions reprise par cette vieille ritournelle, par cette vie faite de saisons, de vacances, de mariages, et de morts. Tout ce tumulte vain de la surface.

(ibid., p. 182)

Similarly, one must assume attitudes and manufacture a personality which will be subservient to the order imposed by the secure life, which will not risk upsetting it by the unexpected spark of originality. Such a man is Herlin, Geneviève's husband, 'cet homme qui pousse en avant un personnage qu'il se compose'. (ibid., p. 63) This, then, is not the answer which Bernis is looking for; 'la vie s'appuie sur autre chose'. (ibid., p. 95)

B. Romantic Love

Bernis believes, for a moment, that he has found the answer to life's enigma in Geneviève, in the possibility of love between two solitary people. But his brief experience in romance does not work, for he is totally unable to understand or deal with the sensitivities of the female heart. As a pilot, Bernis comes from an exclusively masculine world, where facts, duty, and responsibility matter, and emotional sensitivity is banished. Geneviève represents another world, a gentle world in which feelings ignore the harshness of fact. In order to live in such a world, one must soften oneself, allow the feminine aspects of one's nature to rise in precedence over the virile qualities. This leads to weakness, a propensity to lament and to pity oneself, to the selfish indulgence of one's suffering. In Saint-Exupéry's view, romantic love is selfish and emasculating. It imprisons each partner in the egotistical desire to possess the other, and crushes the potential self-realization of both.

Herlin is a lamentably weak man, whose only strength lies in his furious possession of the loved one. The only way in which

he can tie her to him is to make her pity him and to make her
feel guilty for his suffering:

1. 'Cet enfant qu'on a regardé vivre, qu'on a chéri . . .',
   déclamait Herlin. Il désirait se faire plaindre par Geneviève. Ce rôle de père malheureux.   (ibid., p. 72)

And it is Herlin who, in an ecstasy of self-pity, blames his
wife for the death of their child.

Saint-Exupéry always detested the self-regarding attitude of
lovers who fed on pity for each other. His work is full of
references to the weakening effect of sentiment or complaint.
'Pour se faire aimer, il suffit de plaindre', says Rivière in *Vol
de Nuit*. And in *Terre des Hommes*:

2. Plaindre, c'est encore être deux. C'est encore être divisé.
   Mais il existe une altitude des relations où la reconnaissance comme la pitié perdent leur sens.   (p. 131)

Isolated in the desert after a crash, and on the threshold of
death from dehydration, Saint-Exupéry forbids his mechanic
Prévot any show of pity for their fate:

3. Je ne haïssais rien autant, en ce moment-ci, qu'une effusion
   sentimentale . . . Il m'eût été insupportable d'entendre
   geindre. Prévot est un homme.
                      (*Terre des Hommes*, pp. 100, 111)

It is a 'feminine' characteristic to bemoan and bewail, one
that Saint-Exupéry abhors, and sees as all too prevalent in the
state of romantic love. He writes with disdain of the 'slavery'
of love, with horror of the possessiveness of lovers, and with
compassion of those who allow themselves to be seduced into
a life imprisoned in emotion. Such as the two girls he meets in
South America:

4. Alors un imbécile se présente. Pour la première fois des
   yeux si aiguisés se trompent et l'éclairent de belles
   couleurs. L'imbécile, s'il dit des vers, on le croit poète. On
   croit qu'il comprend les parquets troués, on croit qu'il
   aime les mangoustes. On croit que cette confiance le

flatte, d'une vipère qui se dandine, sous la table, entre ses jambes. On lui donne son coeur qui est un jardin sauvage, à lui qui n'aime que les parcs soignés. Et l'imbécile emmène la princesse en esclavage.

(*Terre des Hommes*, p. 53)

At another point in the same book, Saint-Exupéry tells of a young man who killed himself for love, and the reader feels the ripples of the author's indignation:

5. je me souviens d'avoir ressenti en face de cette triste parade une impression non de noblesse mais de misère. Ainsi, derrière ce visage aimable, sous ce crâne d'homme, il n'y avait rien eu, rien. Sinon l'image de quelque sotte petite fille semblable à autres.   (ibid., p. 32)

Courrier Sud, as has been pointed out in the last chapter, contains an element of autobiography. When we read of Jacques Bernis' agonized struggle against the adolescent illusions of love, of his tortuous fight to release himself from the feminine influence in order to achieve manhood in a vocation, we are reading of Saint-Exupéry's own struggle.

Jacques Bernis suffers from the illusion that his love for Geneviève may invest both their lives with a meaning. But he eventually recognizes that he is wrong. Love might offer temporary comfort, but it cannot help find the key to the mystery of life:

6. Mais j'imagine que, pour toi, aimer c'est naître. Tu croiras emporter une Geneviève neuve . . . Et c'est vrai qu'à certaines minutes les mots les plus simples paraissent chargés d'un tel pouvoir, et qu'il est facile de nourrir l'amour . . .

Vivre, sans doute, c'est autre chose.

(*Courrier Sud*, p. 96)

C. Religion

Material comfort, which looks after the body, and romantic love, which satisfies the heart, are both incapable of giving a meaning to life because they indulge the needs of the individual. Saint-Exupéry will have much to say in later works of the destructive effect that individual gratification must have on the spiritual needs of man. If life is to have any meaning, then it is the soul of man which must be nourished.

In the anguish of his re-confirmed solitude, still looking for the 'treasure' which will irradiate his existence, Bernis turns to the Church. But is is clear that his faith has left him. He listens to a sermon, hoping that some word of wisdom might reveal the truth. Before the sermon begins, he admits to himself that he has lost the capacity to believe in God as a law-giver:

1. Il se disait: 'Si je trouve une formule qui m'exprime, qui me rassemble, pour moi ce sera vrai.' Puis il ajoutait avec lassitude: 'Et pourtant, je n'y croirais pas.'

(ibid., p. 130)

Bernis listens to the priest with a growing sense of anger. By the time he has finished, he realizes that instead of offering an answer, religion is merely re-stating the question with an agonized cry of despair:

2. Bernis pensait: 'Quel désespoir! Où est l'acte de foi? Je n'ai pas entendu l'acte de foi, mais un cri parfaitement désespéré.'   (ibid., d. 135)

Saint-Exupéry's biographers all agree that, having been brought up a dutiful and orthodox Catholic, he suffered a religious crisis in adolescence as a result of which he lost his faith. Madame Jean-Jouve, the psycho-analyst, has suggested that he suffered a psychical shock, possibly from the premature death of his young brother (when Saint-Exupéry himself was only seventeen), and that he never recovered.[1] It is likely, therefore, that the religious crisis has its origin in this shattering event. Certainly, when he wrote *Courrier Sud*, he questioned the ability of religion to give weight and substance to human life. Later, he was to create his own religion, the worship of

[1] *The Winged Life*, p. 20.

Man, the germs of which are already present in *Courrier Sud*, and he hardly mentions God as such until his monumental posthumous work *Citadelle* (and even there, the meaning he attaches to the word God remains obscure). At this stage, he already considers the Church to be an irrelevance, and the idea of God to be man's invention. As he wrote in the notebook which he carried with him always, and which was published after his death,

> 3. Et nous l'appelons vérité. Oui, mais vérité en dedans et non en dehors de nous. Dieu est vrai, mais créé peut-être par nous.   (*Carnets*, p. 34)

Yet Saint-Exupéry always retained a religious sensibility. He felt the religious anguish of man's need for the soul's nourishment. Only he regretted that the Catholic faith did not provide that nourishment. The life of the spirit was what mattered pre-eminently for this disappointed monk. 'Je n'aime pas les gens que le bonheur a satisfaits,' he wrote to his mother, 'et qui ne se développeront plus. Il faut être un peu inquiet pour lire autour de soi.' (*Lettres à sa Mère*, p. 157)

If God cannot provide the answer, then it falls on man himself to do so.

D. Escape

Oppressed by the mediocrity of life with which most people seem satisfied (and which is symbolized in Herlin), and longing at the same time for the security which this numb satisfaction brings, Bernis knows that he must struggle against this desire if he is to find a worthwhile reason to live, which he can respect. The petty security of daily business, the love one receives from a woman, the verbose and illusory explanations one receives from religious faith, all these have the effect of turning one inwards upon oneself, of nourishing the solitary ego. Bernis feels obscurely that the answer to life lies on the contrary in expansion, in the release of the ego from its imprisonment, in the flight of the arrow from its bow, and in the fullness of experience dedicated to something more than the mere satisfaction of creature comforts.

In his later work, Saint-Exupéry was to develop this idea of what he calls 'plénitude' and show how men must be helped to recognize their capacity for greatness by subjugating their merely personal desires. But in *Courrier Sud*, the idea has not reached its full expression, and is shown as an incipient but vital need for escape.

1. Fuir, voilà l'important.   (*Courrier Sud*, p. 182)

Bernis cannot understand, interpret, or change the world by remaining within it; it threatens to shackle him with its overwhelmingly crass values. He must escape, flee, soar above it, and see it from a new and different angle. He then becomes a 'fugitive', a 'magician', released from the bonds of conventional existence. There is undeniably a feeling, in this first novel, that Bernis (and Saint-Exupéry, who is only thinly disguised beneath the fiction) is running away. But he is running for a purpose, and that is to allow himself the freedom and opportunity to contemplate, to meditate. It is clear that, but for the loneliness of the cockpit, and the curious and strange view of mankind from a position suspended beneath the stars like a silent, motionless sage, Saint-Exupéry might not have written. Flying revealed the world to him as no other activity could have done, for it placed men and their problems in perspective and offered a unique occasion for reflection.

Saint-Exupéry reserves his most lyrical passages to describe with affection, and almost with sensuality, the sensation of flying:

2. Le bruit s'enfle maintenant, dans les reprises répétées, jusqu'à devenir un milieu dense, presque solide, où le corps se trouve enfermé. Quand le pilote le sent combler en lui quelque chose de jusqu'alors inassouvi, il pense: 'C'est bien'. Puis regarde le capot noir appuyé sur le ciel, à contre-jour, en obusier. Derrière l'hélice, un paysage

d'aube tremble. . . . Maintenant, il résiste moins à l'avion qui cherche à monter, laisse s'épanouir un peu la force que sa main comprime. Il libère d'un mouvement de son poignet chaque vague qui le soulève et qui se propage en lui comme une onde.   (ibid., p. 19–20)
3. L'avion? On avance lentement en creusant son trou dans un cristal dur.   (ibid., p. 28)
4. Six heures d'immobilité et de silence, puis on sort de l'avion comme d'une chrysalide. Le monde est neuf.
                                  (ibid., p. 206)

In *Vol de Nuit*, Saint-Exupéry was to write that the sound of an aeroplane taking off was 'comme le pas formidable d'une armée en marche dans les étoiles', or like 'un chant d'orgue'. (p. 73) There have been other writer-pilots, but only Saint-Exupéry has been able to express the poetry of flying; he is the first poet of aviation. He describes the relationship between the pilot and his aircraft in terms of a mysterious union, like the horse and his jockey. 'Il se découvrait solidement assis dans le ciel . . . Il effleura du doigt un longeron d'acier, et sentit dans le métal ruisseler la vie: le métal ne vibrait pas, mais vivait . . . le travail mystérieux d'une chair vivante.' (*Vol de Nuit*, p. 8) Bernis succeeds in his understanding of his aircraft, where he failed in his understanding of Geneviève. Flying is an escape from love as much as an escape from mundanity.

More than anything else, the solitude of flying gives birth to the thinker, the meditative man who can consider human life and the world from a distance, separated from them, and can slowly reach conclusions. He can weigh the significance of man while free from the necessity of jostling with him, with the peace of 'cette profonde méditation du vol, où l'on savoure une espérance inexplicable'. (*Vol de Nuit*, p. 8) Nowhere is this source of contemplation better expressed than in a passage from *Terre des Hommes*, p. 85:

5. Je sens venir la nuit où l'on s'enferme comme dans un temple. Où l'on s'enferme, aux secrets de rites essentiels, dans une méditation sans secours. Tout ce monde profane s'efface déjà et va disparaître. Tout ce paysage est encore

> nourrie de lumière blonde, mais quelque chose déjà s'en
> évapore. Et je ne connais rien, je dis: rien, qui vaille cette
> heure-là. Et ceux-là me comprennent bien, qui ont subi
> l'inexplicable amour du vol.

The antithesis between the 'profane' world below, and the 'temple' of the heavens is significant. These are the words of a misfit, ill at ease in the world, who seeks to escape not to the confinements of a monastery, but to the meditation of the mystery of man from the vantage point of an empty sky. The fruits of this meditation were *Vol de Nuit*, *Terre des Hommes*, and especially *Pilote de Guerre* and *Citadelle*. And it is a profoundly religious soul, disappointed in religion, which seeks this meditation.

Having left behind him the city with its falseness and confusion, the pilot comes into contact with natural forces; it is a breath of fresh air, a renewal of contact with the elements from which human life has sprung. This idea, embryonic in *Courrier Sud*, will also be developed later, especially in *Terre des Hommes*. Bernis has left the repetitive and facile worries of the town-dweller to read his truth in the stars. The pilot is as intimately linked to nature as is the peasant who ploughs his field. The aeroplane has given twentieth-century man the opportunity to escape *to* reality. There is more than a hint of Rousseau in this idea.

* * * * *

Saint-Exupéry never ceased to be concerned about the meaning of life. Unlike many of his contemporaries, he did not dwell upon the absurdity of human existence, but felt keenly its lack of worthwhile values, values to which a man might dedicate his life. He saw little in an earthbound life to exalt man, to give him something to strive towards, a challenge which might engage the nobility in his nature. He was saddened by the stultified, uninspiring lives of those who, robot-like, followed a pattern. All his life he sought to reveal to men that they had within them the seeds of greatness which, if they allowed them to grow, would enable them to perceive the meaning of the world, and of their place in it. By realizing their potential, giving expression to their present but stifled spirituality, they can create significance out of insipidity. The accent, in *Vol de Nuit*, will be on this *creation* of meaning. *Courrier Sud* presents the problem; the rest of Saint-Exupéry's *oeuvre* attempts to show the way towards solving it.

'Il y a dans toute foule,' says Rivière in *Vol de Nuit*, 'des hommes que l'on ne distingue pas, et qui sont de prodigieux messagers.' (p. 15) Saint-Exupéry would like to see every man recognize the message within him.

3

Vol de Nuit

Vol de Nuit is the fruit of Saint-Exupéry's years in South America among the pioneers of night-flying. It is also the result of his long association with Didier Daurat, to whom the book is dedicated, and on whom the character of Rivière is based.

Published in 1931, with a preface by André Gide, *Vol de Nuit* was an immediate success, and was awarded the Prix Fémina of that year. Reduced from an original manuscript several times as long, it is among the most concise and pregnant of Saint-Exupéry's works, and it established his reputation as an author of note.

The scene of the novel is Buenos Aires. Three night-flights are due to arrive from Chile, Paraguay, and Patagonia, carrying mail which will be assembled in Buenos Aires and then flown to Europe. The Chile and Paraguay flights have arrived; the Patagonian flight is late. As soon as it is realized that all fuel must have been used up, the plane and pilot are declared lost. Nevertheless, the flight to Europe will go ahead as planned. Such is the story of *Vol de Nuit*.

But the real interest of the book lies beyond the obvious tale of adventure. It lies first in the extraordinary personality of Rivière, the Director of the mail-flight company, who carries entire responsibility for the efficiency of the enterprise and the safety of his pilots. Through this character, Saint-Exupéry is able to give us his highly personal ethic of action, the ethic towards which Bernis was groping at the end of *Courrier Sud*. Further, Rivière is the first embodiment, in the Saint-Exupéry *oeuvre*, of the hard, all-powerful visionary leader whose function is to 'forge' men by creating within them the will to surpass themselves, an idea which will be the very foundation of the posthumous *Citadelle*.

And yet Rivière remains human; he is assailed by doubts. The disappearance of the pilot Fabien imposes the question: in the name of what does he force his men to risk their lives? The scene with Fabien's distraught wife emphasizes the question in a particularly painful manner: in the name of what does Rivière demand that his pilots renounce their personal happiness? The ethic of action and the ethic of love are in conflict.

Saint-Exupéry's answer is clear, noble, and imperious. It is not the individual that matters, but the human species. The individual within each man must be ruthlessly suppressed so that the glory of the species might be expressed in some work which will fulfil the aspirations of Mankind, and thus earn Mankind a part of eternity.

Yet this solution, which involves the wilful destruction of happiness and a steely indifference to the sufferings and heartaches of the individual, is a difficult one. The novel ends on a note of victory tinged with sadness, for Rivière recognizes the value of the sweetnesses of life which he must deny his pilots. 'Rivière-le-Grand, Rivière-le-Victorieux, qui porte sa lourde victoire.'

A. Rebirth Through Action

Saint-Exupéry exhorts men to recognize and embrace the nobility within them, to reject the stagnation of a sedentary life, and to allow the imprisoned soul to take wing. This involves a kind of *rebirth*, a setting forth, a beginning, and Saint-Exupéry's texts make much use of the word *naissance* to convey this revolutionary consciousness of a new dimension to life.

In *Terre des Hommes* he writes of the stifling atmosphere of twentieth-century urban life and the dead, artificial existence

B

which it fosters. All men yearn to escape this living death, he says, and be born again:

1. Il est deux cent millions d'hommes, en Europe, qui n'ont point de sens et voudraient naître. L'industrie les a arrachés au langage des lignées paysannes et les a enfermés dans ces ghettos énormes qui ressemblent à des gares de triage encombrées de rames de wagons noirs. Du fond des cités ouvrières, ils voudraient être réveillés.

   (*Terre des Hommes*, p. 135)

And again, in the slim leather notebook which he carried with him everywhere, Saint-Exupéry noted:

2. L'homme doit chercher ailleurs et s'évader (musique, poème, religion, sacrifice, universalité, etc.); le petit ingénieur de l'X avec lequel je déjeunais à Perpignan et qui ne savait rien hors les équations de sa fonction et le poker d'as: quelque chose en lui est manqué.

   (*Carnets*, p. 41)

Jacques Bernis already felt that something was missing from life, something fundamental and essential. He was, however, still an adolescent, tormented by romanticism. He sought his essence in love, and failed. Only when he took to the air did he experience that central sensation of rebirth:

3. Il lui semble naître avec le petit jour qui monte.

   (*Courrier Sud*, p. 21)

But for Bernis the sensation is an expression of his need to escape, and little more. Bernis crystallized the problem; it was for Rivière in *Vol de Nuit* to underline the significance of that escape, and to show the way to rebirth through action.

The pilot Fabien leads a life of action. He has dedicated his life to the achievement of a purpose which lies outside himself, namely the safe delivery of mail by night-flights. Alone in the skies, pitted against the elements and untamed nature, his whole being tensed in constant effort, it is then that he *becomes* someone else; it is by this act of rebirth that he reveals qualities which up to then had existed within him only in potential. Action is therefore a means of *self-knowledge*:

> 4. L'homme se découvre quand il se mesure avec l'obstacle.
> (*Terre des Hommes*, p. 1)

It is for this reason that Saint-Exupéry will not accept ethical objections to the life of action, objections which diminish the achievement of a man's self-discovery by claiming that the delivery of a few letters does not warrant the risk of life and limb. On the contrary, life only begins with action, and that alone would be sufficient justification for acting:

> 5. Si vous aviez objecté à Mermoz, quand il plongeait vers le versant chilien des Andes, avec sa victoire dans le coeur, qu'il se trompait, qu'une lettre de marchand, peut-être, ne valait pas le risque de sa vie, Mermoz eût ri de vous. La vérité, c'est l'homme qui naissait en lui quand il passait les Andes.   (*Terre des Hommes*, p. 133)

It is a recurrent image in Saint-Exupéry to compare man to a tree, spreading its branches outwards and upwards, forever expanding. Just as the tree rises and develops away from the trunk, by virtue of the sap within the trunk, so must man rise and develop away from himself, by virtue of the hidden greatness of which he is capable:

> 6. L'arbre, c'est cette puissance qui lentement épouse le ciel. Ainsi de toi, mon petit homme. . . . Tu es celui qui s'accomplit.   (*Citadelle*, p. 514)

(There is a hint of Sartrean ethics in this idea of man *becoming* himself through his action. When Saint-Exupéry writes in his *Carnets*: 'Ce que *vaut* un homme, c'est tellement *ce qu'il devient*. Moi, je ne sais pas ce qu'il est' (p. 69), one is tempted to hear the voice of Sartre claiming that man cannot be judged by what he *is*, but only by what he *does*. But there, of course, the similarity ends. Sartre would not accept the principle which follows, that freedom lies in the submission to discipline.)

What of those who refuse to expand, who reject the active

life and announce themselves satisfied with what they have?
Saint-Exupéry replies that they cannot possibly know their
inner selves:

7. Et toi qui t'opposes à ce message, comment saurais-tu
ce que tu fais? Tu ignores ce qui serait sorti de toi-même.
Tu te crois continu et essentiel et durable, tu crois que
seuls les sentiments que tu éprouves te sont permis, tu
crois que l'homme que tu portes en toi est achevé, mais
ce mariage mystique, tu ne sais pas de quel oiseau de feu
en toi il déploierait les ailes. Cet empire t'est interdit.
(Carnets, p. 44)

8. Je n'aime pas les sédentaires de coeur. Ceux-là qui
n'échangent rien ne deviennent rien. Et la vie n'aura point
servi à les mûrir. Et le temps coule pour eux comme la
poignée de sable et les perd.   *(Citadelle*, p. 531)

These two passages both touch upon the real purpose of an
active life, as presented in *Vol de Nuit*. Not only does action
reveal man to himself, but, more importantly, it is an act of
creation, which denies the finality of death by *making* something which will last; action brings the triumph of permanence
over transience. 'Le but peut-être ne justifie rien, mais l'action
délivre de la mort.' (p. 66)

Saint-Exupéry knows that man is a temporary creature, and
fears lest he should accept the pessimism which his state
implies. By demanding much of men, by insisting on the
resolute effort of a life of action which brings men in contact
with the world and forces them to surpass themselves in order
to conquer it, he hopes that men will realize their potential
nobility. He says that men do not want a superficial happiness,
but a substance and weight, and a certain eternity. Their
anguish derives from a lack of identity and a lack of self-
knowledge. The inexorable passage of time saddens, debili-
tates, and emasculates them. Saint-Exupéry's message to men
is that their taste for permanence can only be satisfied by creating something of lasting value. 'L'instinct essentiel est l'instinct
de la permanence.' The life of action allows them to do
this.

Rivière is the embodiment of the exhortation to surpass oneself. He demands more of his pilots than would appear humanly reasonable, in the knowledge that they will thereby discover themselves and fulfil their desire for permanence:

9. Il pensa encore pour se rassurer: 'Tous ces hommes, je les aime, mais ce n'est pas eux que je combats. C'est ce qui passe par eux . . .'
   Son coeur battait des coups rapides, qui le faisaient souffrir.
   'Je ne sais pas si ce que j'ai fait est bon. Je ne sais pas l'exacte valeur de la vie humaine, ni de la justice, ni du chagrin. Je ne sais pas exactement ce que vaut la joie d'un homme. Ni une main qui tremble. Ni la pitié, ni la douceur . . .'
   Il rêva:
   'La vie se contredit tant, on se débrouille comme on peut avec la vie. . . . Mais durer, mais créer, échanger son corps périssable . . .'   (*Vol de Nuit*, p. 36)

So, the meaning of action is to exchange our ephemeral self against a creation which may last longer than we ourselves can. 'Le bonheur est de s'échanger et de durer dans l'objet de sa création.' (*Citadelle*, p. 612)

In order to explain the importance of Saint-Exupéry's concept of rebirth through action, and of its consequent denial of death, we have run the risk of chronological infidelity. At the time of writing *Vol de Nuit*, Saint-Exupéry was certain that a life of action was the way towards self-realization, but he was by no means sure how to justify the hardship which such a life would entail. We should have to wait for *Terre des Hommes* for the full ring of conviction of a philosophy which in *Vol de Nuit*, despite appearances, is still tentative. Rivière is beset by doubts. The novel is the story of a night in the life of Rivière, a night tormented by his inability to explain the liberating and renewing effects of the sacrifices he demands from his pilots. The transcendental value of self-enrichment through action has not yet been fully articulated.

'Nous agissons toujours comme si quelquechose dépassait,

en valeur, la vie humaine,' muses Rivière. 'Mais quoi?'
Hesitantly, he perceives that he struggles not to save men as
they are, but to save what they can *become*;

> 10. Il existe peut-être quelque chose d'autre à sauver et de
> plus durable; peut-être est-ce à sauver cette part-là de
> l'homme que Rivière travaille? Sinon l'action ne se
> justifie pas.   (*Vol de Nuit*, p. 54)

Once more this insistence on *durability*.

Not only does Rivière demand a great deal from his pilots
without being able fully to explain why, but they too give of
themselves totally, without understanding why. Not one mem-
ber of the team for one moment considers deserting his fellows
to find his own personal destiny outside. Each gives himself to
the work of the community of which he is part. Each obeys
Rivière without question. Rivière has created the community,
he is its soul, its law. They know obscurely, in the depths of
their being, that they owe to Rivière the rebirth which their
active life has made possible. They owe him a debt which
passes language. They therefore have a duty towards him, a
duty towards each other to respect the community which he
has created, and a duty towards their *métier*. This threefold
duty implies their fundamental *liberty*. It is easy to see how this
seeming paradox hides no contradiction in the thought of
Saint-Exupéry. He has already said that the real imprisonment
is (a) introspection, the static, narcissistic concern with self,
and (b) its corollary, the culpable acceptance of mediocrity.
Duty towards others can only be a liberating influence, releasing the shackles of self-absorption. As André Gide wrote in
his preface to *Vol de Nuit*:

> 11. Je lui sais gré particulièrement d'éclairer cette vérité
> paradoxale, pour moi d'une importance psychologique
> considérable: que le bonheur de l'homme n'est pas dans
> la liberté, mais dans l'acceptation d'un devoir.   (p.2)

The man who has no duties, no ties, is perhaps free, but his
freedom is 'la liberté de n'être point'. (*Pilote de Guerre*, p. 184)

Duties place a man in chains, yet free him at the same time. 'Chaque obligation fait devenir' (ibid.) Real freedom is not (to use an image of Saint-Exupéry) that of a stone lying loose in a field, but that of the stone which has found its place in the vault.

Freedom is not a right, it is a reward, it relies on the acceptance of discipline. Freedom is not independence, quite the contrary. Freedom is the total embracing of a discipline.

The pilots feel responsible towards each other and towards Rivière, who himself carries the most heavy responsibility of all; 'il est responsable d'un ciel entier'. (p. 29)

Saint-Exupéry's closest friend, whom he admired above all men, and with whom he seems to have felt an 'elective affinity', was the famous airman Guillaumet. He later wrote that one of the sources of Guillaumet's greatness lay in his acknowledgement of responsibility:

12. Sa grandeur, c'est de se sentir responsable. Responsable de lui, du courrier, et des camarades qui espèrent. Il tient dans ses mains leur peine ou leur joie. Responsable de ce qui se bâtit de neuf, là-bas, chez les vivants, à quoi il doit participer. Responsable un peu du destin des hommes, dans la mesure de son travail.
    Il fait parti des êtres larges qui acceptent de couvrir de larges horizons de leur feuillage. Etre homme, c'est précisément être responsable. . . . C'est sentir, en posant sa pierre, que l'on contribue à bâtir le monde.
                                                        (*Terre des Hommes*, p. 31)

As the fox said to the Little Prince: 'tu es responsable de ta rose'.

The acceptance of duty implies the control of the emotions, which Saint-Exupéry considers self-regarding, self-indulgent, and weak. We have already seen the contempt with which he draws the character of Herlin in *Courrier Sud*, a man vitiated by sentiment. He has more compassion for the weakness of Robineau, the lonely inspector who wants so much to feel the the warmth of friendship, but he condemns a display of emotion with equal vigour. 'Aimez ceux que vous commandez,' Rivière says to Robineau, 'mais sans le leur dire.' (p. 25)

When it is known that Fabien is lost, Robineau sees Rivière alone, bearing the full weight of the disaster in solitary anguish. He feels pity for the man, wants to reach out and comfort him:

13. Puis lui vint l'image d'un Rivière enfermé, là, dans son bureau, et qui lui avait dit: 'Mon vieux . . .' Jamais homme n'avait, à ce point, manqué d'appui. Robineau éprouva pour lui un grand pitié. Il remuait dans sa tête quelques phrases obscurément destinées à plaindre, à soulager. Un sentiment qu'il jugeait très beau l'animait.
(p. 69)

But Rivière rejects the poor man's proffered friendship. There is no place in an active life for whining.

The last moments of Fabien are described in a beautifully moving passage, which is none the less devoid of sentiment. It ends with a paragraph which makes clear that Fabien remained true to his 'rebirth' to the death, and did not once degenerate into self-pity:

14. Rivière pense qu'un poste radio l'écoute encore. Seule relie encore Fabien au monde une onde musicale, une modulation mineure. Pas une plainte. Pas un cri. Mais le son le plus pur qu'ait jamais formé le désespoir.
(p. 62)

Rivière is the incarnation of an idea to which Saint-Exupéry dedicated almost the whole of his posthumous work *Citadelle*, the idea of the visionary leader, the 'chef' who must channel the potentialities of his men with pitiless rigour. He must make them fulfil themselves, even if it be in spite of themselves:

15. Parce que les événements, on les commande, pensait Rivière, et ils obéissent, et on crée. Et les hommes sont de pauvres choses, et on les crée aussi. Ou bien on les écarte lorsque le mal passe par eux.   (p. 34)

To fulfil the function of a *chef*, Rivière cannot allow himself any of the weaknesses which he condemns in others, any of the human tenderness which Robineau so covets. He must appear hard, harsh, remorseless – but only appear so:

16. Pour se faire aimer, il suffit de plaindre. Je ne plains guère, ou je le cache. J'aimerais bien pourtant m'entourer de l'amitié et de la douceur humaines. Un médecin, dans son métier, les rencontre. Mais ce sont les événements que je sers. Il faut que je forge les hommes pour qu'ils les servent.   (p. 41)

Rivière forms, fashions, shapes the destinies of his men. He demands the impossible in order to serve a higher cause. Weakness, failure, pity, must all be condemned without argument. For him, as we have seen, the essential effort is to create, 'd'échanger son corps périssable'. He creates the will to achieve, offers his men solidity. And they know that without a leader like Rivière, their energies would be dissipated and rootless. 'Je les sauve par ma rigueur.' (*Citadelle*). It is a cardinal concept in Saint-Exupéry's ethic of action that the leader and the led are equally dependent upon each other. The leader fills a *need* in men:

17. Nous chercher un chef, c'est, pour nous, nous chercher nous-mêmes. Un chef c'est celui qui a infiniment besoin des autres. Et nous voulons qu'on ait besoin de nous. Personne ici n'a besoin de nous. Nous faisons antichambre pour offrir nos services. Un chef, c'est celui qui nous *attire* au lieu d'acheter comme un octroi de faveurs l'acceptation de notre aide. Voyez Mermoz, la joie des hommes quand il en est beaucoup exigé.
                                    (*Carnets*, p. 23)

The question inevitably arises whether we can wholly admire an ethic which condones blatant injustice. Rivière's summary treatment of Rolet is almost cruel. An old man, a faithful worker, Rolet has committed an error, the first in his many years of service. Rivière dismisses him. He will not listen to the old man's heart-rending pleas. We know, and Rivière himself knows, that he has been unjust. But he is indifferent to the moral of individual justice:

18. Le règlement, pensait Rivière, est semblable aux rites d'une religion qui semblent absurdes mais façonnent les hommes. Il était indifférent à Rivière de paraître juste ou injuste. Peut-être ces mots-là n'avaient-ils même pas de sens pour lui. Les petits bourgeois des petites villes tournent le soir autour de leur kiosque à musique, et Rivière pensait: 'Juste ou injuste envers eux, cela n'a pas de sens: ils n'existent pas.' L'homme était pour lui une cire vierge qu'il fallait pétrir. Il fallait donner une âme à cette matière, lui créer une volonté. Il ne pensait pas les asservir par cette dureté, mais les lancer hors d'eux-mêmes. . . .

. . . 'Ces hommes-là sont heureux parce qu'ils aiment ce qu'ils font, et ils l'aiment parce que je suis dur.' Il faisait peut-être souffrir, mais procurait aussi aux hommes de fortes joies. 'Il faut les pousser, pensait-il, vers une vie forte qui entraîne des souffrances et des joies, mais qui seule compte.'   (pp. 18–19)

Rivière has an unshakeable faith in his work, a faith which is certainly *religious* in its exclusivity. It is clear from the passage above that his convictions are almost those of a fanatic. The ethic of action is an *absolute* which must admit no compromise. We saw in the last chapter that Bernis turned from the Christian faith because it taught despair. In *Vol de Nuit*, Rivière suggests an alternative religion, just as demanding, but one that teaches construction, creation, and hope – the religion of Mankind, 'le caractère sacré de l'aventure'. Hence relative concepts of justice and injustice can hold no sway before the absolute of the new religion:

19. Toute justice est arbitraire: celle de l'égalité – mais celles-ci flatte les larves. Il ne s'agit pas d'être juste mais de créer l'homme.   (*Carnets*, p. 68)

The question of justice is therefore irrelevant. One must only consider which ethical structure most favours the releasing of the inner nobility of men.

B. The Conflict Between Action and Happiness

If liberating action is an absolute in Rivière's canon, quiet personal happiness is an absolute which challenges it; the two ideas are in violent opposition, and can admit no synthesis. *Vol de Nuit* is the story of the conflict between these two absolutes, the one represented by Rivière, the other by Simone Fabien.

Courrier Sud posed a question. Is it possible to reconcile the feminine values of tenderness and comfort with the severe masculine demands of action? *Vol de Nuit* gives the answer: it is not.

Not that Rivière (and Saint-Exupéry) is unresponsive to 'les douceurs de la vie'. He muses upon them, questions whether he will ever be allowed them in his old age, and is profoundly and painfully aware of their powerful attraction. So too does the pilot Fabien reflect upon the calm, undemanding happiness hidden beneath the roofs below him as he flies; there is some envy in his thoughts:

1. En descendant moteur au ralenti sur San-Julien, Fabien se sentit las. Tout ce qui fait douce la vie des hommes grandissait vers lui: leurs maisons, leurs petits cafés, les arbres de leur promenade. Il était semblable à un conquérant, au soir de ses conquêtes, qui se penche sur les terres de l'empire, et découvre l'humble bonheur des hommes. Fabien avait besoin de déposer ses armes, de ressentir sa lourdeur et ses courbatures, on est riche aussi de ses misères, et d'être ici un homme simple, qui regarde par la fenêtre une vision désormais immuable. Ce village minuscule, il l'eût accepté; après avoir choisi on se contente du hasard de son existence et on peut l'aimer. Il vous borne comme l'amour. Fabien eût désiré vivre ici longtemps, prendre sa part ici d'éternité, car les petites villes, où il vivait une heure, et les jardins clos de vieux murs, qu'il traversait, lui semblaient éternels de durer en dehors de lui . . . Et Fabien pensait aux amitiés, aux filles tendres, à l'intimité des nappes blanches, à tout ce qui, lentement, s'apprivoise pour l'éternité.   (pp. 6–7)

Fabien feels the gnawing need for permanence, and suspects, for a moment, that the need could be satisfied by hiding himself away in a cotton-wool happiness. But Rivière is there to disabuse him. And Fabien realizes, by the end of the passage, that constant tenderness must be denied him:

2. Ce village défendait, par sa seule immobilité, le secret de ses passions, ce village refusait sa douceur: il eût fallu renoncer à l'action pour la conquérir.   (ibid.)

Saint-Exupéry was never impervious to the seductive charms of a house full of happiness, rooted and solid in its soil. But he also knew that he would always be stifled by a stagnant contentment which did not aspire to something greater. For him, such happiness could only cradle the body, soften the soul.

Simone Fabien knows that there is a significant part of her husband which she cannot share, which belongs only to himself and to Rivière:

3. Elle connaissait les sourires de cet homme, ses précautions d'amant, mais non, dans l'orage, ses divines colères. Elle le chargeait de tendres liens: de musique, d'amour, de fleurs; mais, à l'heure de chaque départ, ces liens, sans qu'il en parût souffrir, tombaient.   (p. 37)

And after he has left:

Elle restait là. Elle regardait, triste, ces fleurs, ces livres, cette douceur, qui n'étaient pour lui qu'un fond de mer.
(p. 39)

One of the great climaxes of the novel is the meeting between Simone Fabien and Rivière, the clash of absolutes. It is at this point that the confrontation of opposites is presented with all its pathos:

4. Il était parvenu à cette frontière où se pose, non le problème d'une petite détresse particulière, mais celui-là même de l'action. En face de Rivière se dressait, non la femme de Fabien, mais un autre sens de la vie. Rivière ne pouvait qu'écouter, que plaindre cette petite voix, ce chant tellement triste, mais ennemi. Car ni l'action, ni le

> bonheur individuel n'admettent le partage: ils sont en
> conflit. Cette femme parlait elle aussi au nom d'un monde
> absolu et de ses devoirs et de ses droits . . . elle exigeait
> son bien et elle avait raison. Et lui aussi, Rivière, avait
> raison, mais il ne pouvait rien opposer à la vérité de cette
> femme. (p. 53)

Rivière wonders what it is that can justify the denial of personal happiness. One does not stop constructing a bridge because one of the workers is killed in the process. Something there is which has a higher value than mere human life. But what?

5. 'Ces hommes, pensait-il, qui vont peut-être disparaître, auraient pu vivre heureux.' Il voyait des visages penchés dans le sanctuaire d'or des lampes du soir. 'Au nom de quoi les en ai-je tirés?' Au nom de quoi les a-t-il arrachés au bonheur individuel? La première loi n'est-elle pas de protéger ces bonheurs-là? Mais lui-même les brise.
(p. 54)

The higher value which Rivière perceives is, as we have seen, the value of permanence, which permits him to snatch from the transitoriness of human existence a creation of lasting worth. Such a creation may offer no comfort to Simone Fabien, may contribute little to individual happiness, but the *chef* is less concerned with the individual than with the species Man. As the Incas left behind them an eloquent testimony of their greatness, so Rivière will make his pilots leave behind them something which surpasses their personal needs. Even if they are killed, as Fabien is, the value of their work will remain:

6. 'Aimer, aimer seulement, quelle impasse!' Rivière eut l'obscur sentiment d'un devoir plus grand que celui d'aimer. Ou bien il s'agissait aussi d'une tendresse, mais si différente des autres. Une phrase lui revint: 'Il s'agit de les rendre éternels.' Où avait-il lu cela? 'Ce que vous poursuivez en vous-même meurt.' Il revit un temple au dieu soleil des anciens Incas du Pérou. Ces pierres droites sur la montagne. Que resterait-il, sans elles, d'une civilisation puissante. . . . Le conducteur de peuples d'autrefois,

s'il n'eut peut-être pas pitié de la souffrance de l'homme, eut pitié, immensément, de sa mort. Non de sa mort individuelle, mais pitié de l'espèce qu'effacera la mer de sable.   (p. 55)

C. Suppression of the Individual

Man, in order to assert himself and create his own permanence, must embrace a life of action which of necessity excludes all right to personal happiness. Yet within every man there lurks the individual part of his nature, that proud spirit of independence which claims its right to happiness and security, and which refuses to adhere to laws imposed by others. It is this individual that we must root out and conquer. Saint-Exupéry rejects the cult of the individual as leading only to failure and weakness. He exhorts men to suppress and destroy their instinct towards egotism, to struggle to achieve self-mastery.

Action is thus made doubly strenuous; not only is it a battle with the forces of nature, with the elements, but there is also this corresponding inner battle with oneself. Rivière's purpose is to help his men, *in spite of themselves*, achieve mastery over their debilitating individuality:

1. il ne pensait pas les asservir par cette dureté, mais les lancer hors d'eux-mêmes.   (p. 19)

Action is to go beyond possibilities, to fight against adverse forces, to conquer a resistance, but also to forget oneself, to offer oneself without restriction. Only then may one accomplish that transcendence from the *Individual* to the *Man* wherein lies the salvation of the species:

2. Il est donc quelqu'un en moi que je combats pour me grandir. Il a fallu ce voyage difficile pour que je distingue ainsi en moi, tant bien que mal, l'individu que je combats de l'homme qui grandit. Je ne sais ce que vaut l'image qui me vient, mais je me dis: l'individu n'est qu'une route. L'Homme qui l'emprunte compte seul.
                                        (*Pilote de Guerre*, p. 214)

The man who lives (and does not merely exist), must engage in permanent battle with himself, must seek to control and master those natural dispositions towards egotism:

3. Je combattrai pour l'Homme. Contre ses ennemis. Mais aussi contre moi-même.   (ibid., p. 242)

The Little Prince echoes this conclusion in simpler terms. On his travels to different planets in the universe, he visits one inhabited by a king, one by a narcissist, one by a drunkard, one by a businessman, and one by a lamplighter. They all appear ridiculous to the tiny observer, save the last; the lamp-lighter absorbed in his ceaseless task:

4. Celui-là, se dit le petit prince, tandis qu'il poursuivait plus loin son voyage, celui-là serait méprisé par tous les autres, par le roi, par le vaniteux, par le buveur, par le businessman. Cependant, c'est le seul qui ne me paraisse pas ridicule. C'est, peut-être, parcequ'il s'occupe d'autre chose que de soi-même.   (Le Petit Prince, p. 52)

In Vol de Nuit we are shown the sharp, bright contrast between the man who has accomplished the total suppression of his individuality, and the man who has not. Rivière, clearly, is the man 'in transcendence'. He knows that his pilots will only become men when they no longer belong to themselves, as he no longer belongs to himself. He may appear implacable, harsh, strong, invulnerable, but a constant effort is demanded of him to overcome his own weaknesses, which are not eradicated, but kept in control. He feels for Simone Fabien, whose happiness crumples before his eyes. He feels for the old Rolet, whom he is forced to dismiss and whose life is thus summarily deprived of its structure. He feels the need for tenderness, and muses whether he will ever experience it. He knows the meaning of pity. But Rivière is the perfect expression of a man who is in control of himself, who is stretched to the limit and tuned to surpass himself. He has made himself invulnerable.

The man who remains obstinately an individual is the inspector Robineau. He is vulnerable because he succumbs to his weaknesses. Herlin in *Courrier Sud* was vulnerable; he was dominated by the weaknesses of possession and self-pity. Even Jacques Bernis was vulnerable, torn by the demands of love. In both cases, the weakness of the character sprang from the desire to satisfy the needs of the individual, needs which prevent transcendence towards something higher. Only at the end of the novel did Bernis begin to release himself from his individuality.

Robineau is the most clearly drawn example of a man who has failed. He is sad and lonely, with only the dignity of his exalted position as an inspector to sustain him. He indulges his sadness, advertises it, suffers acutely from the necessity to remain aloof and separate from the pilots whose friendship he craves, 'car un inspecteur n'est pas créé pour les délices de l'amour, mais pour la rédaction de rapports'. (*Vol de Nuit*, p. 17) He has tried to 'join in' by proposing suggestions for the improvement of the service, but Rivière replied with a cruel letter: 'L'Inspecteur Robineau est prié de nous fournir, non des poèmes, mais des rapports.' (ibid.) This man who aches for tenderness, for a hand on his shoulder, is constrained to fulfil a function which makes such tenderness impossible; his job is to discover any faults or lapses in the pilots, and to punish them for it. Unlike Rivière or the pilots, who accept their duty to forget themselves, Robineau finds the loneliness too painful to bear.

He is not very intelligent, does not understand the higher purpose of Rivière's plan:

5. Un règlement établi par Rivière était, pour Rivière, connaissance des hommes; mais pour Robineau n'existait plus qu'une connaissance du règlement.   (ibid.)
   Il ne pense rien, disait de lui Rivière, ça lui évite de penser faux.   (ibid., p. 18)

The crisis in Robineau's life occurs when, overwhelmed with loneliness, he seeks the friendship of the pilot Pellerin:

6. Or Robineau ce soir était las. Il venait de découvrir, en face de Pellerin vainqueur, que sa propre vie était grise.

Il venait surtout de découvrir que lui, Robineau, malgré
son titre d'inspecteur et son autorité, valait moins que cet
homme rompu de fatigue, tassé dans l'angle de la voiture,
les yeux clos et les mains noires d'huile. Pour la première
fois, Robineau admirait. Il avait besoin de le dire. Il avait
besoin surtout de se gagner une amitié.   (ibid., p. 19)

Robineau invites Pellerin to dine with him, explaining the
sudden invitation by his need for a little conversation to lighten
the burden of his hard and solitary position. In other words, he
pleads for the pilot's pity, as Herlin pleaded for Geneviève's.
In Saint-Exupéry's canon there are few crimes more morally
heinous than the pursuit of pity. It is Robineau's undoing.

The inspector is showing Pellerin his collection of geological
specimens when Rivière sends for him. Robineau has never
shown anyone his rocks before:

7. Seules, dans la vie, avaient été douces pour lui, les pierres.
                                                    (ibid., p. 23)

Rivière sees his whole purpose threatened by the inspector's
weakness. Were he to allow an intimate friendship to flourish,
the imperious and destructive needs of the individual might
interfere with the pilot's duty towards his profession. It must
at all costs be stopped. Rivière summons Robineau before
him.

Rivière's reprimand is abrupt and pitiless. You may be
required to send that pilot on a dangerous mission tomorrow,
he says; he will have to obey you. And do not think for one
moment that he will obey you out of affection for your person:

8. — Si c'est par amitié qu'ils vous obéissent, vous les dupez.
   Vous n'avez droit vous-même à aucun sacrifice.
                                                    (ibid., p. 25)

The *chef* forces Robineau to sever any incipient emotional
ties with the pilot in the cruellest possible fashion. Robineau
will issue a punishment for a non-existent fault, which will kill
any trust that Pellerin may have been on the point of feeling.

You may feel affection for the pilots, says Rivière, but you must show none:

9. — Je vais vous mettre à votre place, Robineau. Si vous êtes las, ce n'est pas à ces hommes de vous soutenir. Vous êtes le chef. Votre faiblesse est ridicule. Écrivez.
   — Je . . .
   — Écrivez: L'Inspecteur Robineau inflige au pilote Pellerin telle sanction pour tel motif. . . . Vous trouverez un motif quelconque.
   — Monsieur le Directeur!
   — Faites comme si vous compreniez, Robineau. Aimez ceux que vous commandez. Mais sans le leur dire.

   (ibid., p. 25)

Robineau had thought to enrich his life with a little human affection. But he was misguided. His life would, on the contrary, have been impoverished, for the level of human endeavour would have been brought down to the satisfaction of mere personal needs. The way to salvation lies in strenuous effort *at the cost of* individual satisfaction. The individual, turned in upon himself, refusing the ascension which is offered, is the enemy of man:

10. dès que l'on enferme l'homme en lui-même, il devient pauvre. Dès qu'il *se* sert.   (*Carnets*, p. 24)

Saint-Exupéry has a special word for this constant effort of the individual to break out of the imprisonment of his own selfishness, a word which he uses more in his later work: *ferveur*. The religious implications of the word, as with so much of Saint-Exupéry's vocabulary, are again evident. The individual is 'profane', man is 'sacred', action is the continual striving which denies the one in order to release the other.

*   *   *   *   *

The moral of *Vol de Nuit* hinges on the conflict between action and personal happiness (Rivière *v.* Simone Fabien), and between self-abnegation and selfishness (Rivière *v.* Robineau).

Both are different aspects of the same confrontation, and both echo the original conflict of *Courrier Sud*, between masculine stoicism and feminine tenderness. The world of Saint-Exupéry is beginning to assume the shape of a world of clearly defined opposites, of good and bad, sacred and profane, aspiration and stagnation. It has the clarity of a religion.

Action requires that the individual should realize himself through the desire of something *beyond* himself, that he should control his weaknesses, restrain his egotism, in order to contribute to a community whose value will be measured in terms of his accomplishment.

4

Terre des Hommes

Saint-Exupéry's first two books were a mixture of fiction and autobiography. In *Terre des Hommes* (1939) he abandons the novel form altogether to write a series of reflections on the human condition which repeat and develop some of the themes of *Courrier Sud* and *Vol de Nuit*. In particular, the nature of the community to which Rivière and his pilots sacrificed their personal happiness is here clarified and explained. The book is in effect one long meditation in flight, during which essential truths are illustrated and confirmed by anecdotes drawn from Saint-Exupéry's own experience.

The aircraft is a supreme instrument of analysis. It reveals first of all the overwhelming *sterility* of the earth, and the *fragile miracle* of man's presence on it. Human endeavour alone can give meaning to the huge senselessness of the world. In turn, man is enriched by his contact with the world, if he seeks not to plunder it, but to understand it, and to understand his place in it in terms of evolutionary history.

The vocational life, a life of action, reveals the importance of companionship to men, and especially the profound *brotherhood of men* tied in obligation to each other. Such men contrast vividly with those dedicated to the pursuit of material gain, or satisfied with the mediocrity of a sedentary life. The real anguish of the human condition is to be 'free', that is, tied to no one, with no responsibilities or obligations. Such is the anguish of the slave Bark, when he has been given his freedom by those to whom he was once tied. Responsibility towards one's fellows affords man his dignity.

The tragedy of human existence is that there are so many

men who are unaware that they have the seeds of greatness within them, that there is a higher plane of life to which they could aspire by giving of themselves. For lack of spiritual nourishment, their lives are fed on illusions. With the enthusiasm and urgency of a crusader, the author seeks to reveal to men *their* truth.

A. The Aeroplane

It would be a gross injustice to refer to Saint-Exupéry as the 'writer of the air', as if the celebration of flying were his only purpose. The truth is quite otherwise. For Saint-Exupéry the aeroplane is a tool, as the chisel is for the carpenter. It is a means to an end, not an end in itself. The pilot is a contemplative man, for whom the aeroplane is an instrument of study:

1. La terre nous en apprend plus long sur nous que tous les livres. Parce qu'elle nous résiste. L'homme se découvre quand il se mesure avec l'obstacle. Mais, pour l'atteindre, il lui faut un outil. Il lui faut un rabot, ou une charrue. Le paysan, dans son labour, arrache peu à peu quelques secrets à la nature, et la vérité qu'il dégage est universelle. De même l'avion, l'outil des lignes aériennes, mêle l'homme à tous les vieux problèmes. (*Terre des Hommes*, p. 1)

Thus the opening lines of *Terre des Hommes*. The author returns to this statement time and again, emphasizing that the pilot, like the peasant, is brought into contact with nature, a contact denied the town-dweller (cf. *Courrier Sud*). The famous pilot Henri Guillaumet is no mere manipulator of levers, but a poet, a philosopher, an observer. Flying upsets all our established concepts of distance, of time, and especially of man's relative place in the world; it uncovers simplicity beneath accustomed complexity, affords a new angle of vision, re-unites men with the essential truths of life which have lain buried for so long:

2. L'avion n'est pas un but: c'est un outil. Un outil comme la charrue. (ibid., p. 33)

3. Au delà de l'outil, et à travers lui, c'est la vieille nature que nous retrouvons, celle du jardinier, du navigateur, ou du poète.   (ibid., p. 35)

4. Le pilote ferme les mains sur les commandes et, peu à peu, dans ses paumes creuses, il reçoit ce pouvoir comme un don. Les organes de métal des commandes, à mesure que ce don lui est accordé, se font les messagers de sa puissance.   (ibid., p. 36)

5. Il ne s'agit point ici d'aviation. L'avion, ce n'est pas une fin, c'est un moyen. Ce n'est pas pour l'avion que l'on risque sa vie. Ce n'est pas non plus pour la charrue que le paysan laboure. Mais, par l'avion, on quitte les villes et leurs comptables, et l'on retrouve une vérité paysanne. On fait un travail d'homme et l'on connaît des soucis d'homme. On est en contact avec le vent, avec les étoiles, avec la nuit, avec le sable, avec la mer. On ruse avec les forces naturelles. On attend l'aube comme le jardinier attend le printemps. On attend l'escale comme une terre promise, et l'on cherche sa vérité dans les étoiles.

(ibid., p. 115)

B. The Fragile Miracle

1. L'avion est une machine sans doute, mais quel instrument d'analyse! Cet instrument nous a fait découvrir le vrai visage de la terre.   (ibid., p. 37)

What is the image of the earth that the pilot sees when he has left it? It is that of an empty planet, apparently devoid of life: a desert of sterility. It is a vision of volcanic deadness, 'un désert de lune et de pierres'. And what of the pilot's place in this emptiness? 'La terre est vide. Il n'est plus d'hommes quand on observe à des kilomètres de distance.' (*Pilote de Guerre* p. 72) The pilot is profoundly alone, suspended between stars and sand, above him a changeless sky, below him a cold and desolate planet. He has the sensation of seeing the world in a pre-human state, as if the human race had never walked upon its surface. It is a naked, stony, hostile place.

So, if the aeroplane is an instrument of analysis, the truth it initially reveals is the vision of an empty planet wiped clean of human presence; it is a means of returning to times so distant that life was unknown. The pilot is like the first molecule of living matter to appear on the earth.

2. Je n'étais rien qu'un mortel égaré entre du sable et des étoiles, conscient de la seule douceur de respirer.
(ibid., p. 44)

What signs there are of human life are so minute as to ...derline the pathetic insignificance of the human being:

3. Les hommes occupent peu de place dans l'immensité des terres.   (*Pilote de Guerre*, p. 91)

And their civilizations could be so cleanly and simply annihilated by a tiny volcanic eruption:

4. . . . hasardés comme ils sont sur une lave encore tiède, et déjà menacés par les sables futurs, menacés par les neiges. Leurs civilisations ne sont que fragiles dorures: un volcan les efface, une mer nouvelle, un vent de sable.
(*Terre des Hommes*, p. 40)

Fragile though the human presence on earth may be, it is a miracle, a source of wonder and amazement. However insignificant men may appear from the sky, the fact that they are there at all is to be celebrated:

5. Mais le plus merveilleux était qu'il y eût là, debout sur le dos rond de la planète, entre ce linge aimanté et ces étoiles, une conscience d'homme dans laquelle cette pluie pût se réfléchir comme dans un miroir. Sur une assise de minéraux un songe est un miracle.   (ibid., p. 43)

At no point is the miracle of human life so wonderful as when Saint-Exupéry and his mechanic are lost in the desert, near death from lack of water, and so far from any hint of human presence as to be abandoned on a foreign planet. Suddenly, they see the proof that men have not ceased to exist – footprints in the sand!

6. Nous sommes sauvés, il y a des traces dans le sable! Ah! nous avions perdu la piste de l'espèce humaine, nous

étions tranchés d'avec la tribu, nous nous étions retrouvés seuls au monde, oubliés par une migration universelle, et voici que nous découvrons, imprimés dans le sable, les pieds miraculeux de l'homme.   (ibid., p. 119)

And when the Arab appears with water, water without which life, however important, is impossible, he is an Archangel, he is the ambassador of Mankind:

> 7. C'est un miracle . . . Il marche vers nous sur le sable, comme un dieu sur la mer . . . L'Arabe nous a simplement regardés. Il a pressé, des mains, sur nos épaules, et nous lui avons obéi. Nous nous sommes étendus. Il n'y a plus ici ni races, ni langages, ni divisions . . . Il y a ce nomade pauvre qui a posé sur nos épaules des mains d'archange.
> (ibid., p. 121)

Man is seen as a miracle triumphant over the sterility of the mineral, inorganic world. He is the denial of the lifelessness which the planet seems to impose. And he *must* be saved. Hence the high missionary zeal with which Saint-Exupéry exhorts men to recognize their special status on a dead planet, and to avoid leading lives which are as dead as the stones on which their houses stand. Hence the author's love of men and the spring of his profound Humanism.

So keen is Saint-Exupéry to impress upon men the uniquely privileged position which evolution has conferred upon them that again and again he returns to the stark opposition between a sterile earth and the creative marvel of life. In *Le Petit Prince* he presents the Little Prince, a fragile spark of life, against a décor of dead planets turning pointlessly in infinity; one solitary rose among lifeless rocks and chasms; the spring of life in a desert of inanimate matter. The minute and graceful prince is a potent challenge to the staggering emptiness of the universe.

Time and again, Saint-Exupéry seems to dwell upon images of sterility; even his illustrations for *Le Petit Prince* show that he sees the world as an asteroid. Lifeless words abound in his descriptions of the earth – mineral, lava, sand, salt, rock.

R.-M. Albérès has made the interesting suggestion that Saint-Exupéry is haunted by images of sterility, and that he is obsessed with the need to assert the fertility of man. Albérès further implies that Saint-Exupéry would be a fitting study for pschoanalysis, since his work betrays a desperate need for paternity, and that his only offspring was a literary one – *Le Petit Prince*.[1]

Be that as it may, it is important to note the vividness of this opposition in imagery, since upon it is founded the Humanism of *Terre des Hommes* and of *Pilote de Guerre*. That the opposition was never far from Saint-Exupéry's consciousness is attested by the frequency of similar references in his private notebook, which has since been published:

8. La vie est une résistance aux gains de l'entropie.
(Carnets, p. 173)

The very existence of life is a source of infinite wonder itself. But more than that, the special qualities of life that man has evolved – and which seem to go beyond man – are as precious gold to Saint-Exupéry; consciousness, creativity, nobility of soul, these intangibles of which every man is a potential expression, but which too often lie submerged beneath habit and mediocrity.

These qualities are not God-given in the sense that they are bestowed. They are *evolved*. Saint-Exupéry's vision of the world and of man's place in it leads inevitably to a global view of the entire history of mankind, and of the cardinal role played by evolutionary progress. Not only have we evolved our appearance, our bipedal stature, our molecular structure, from creatures who existed millions of years before us, but even the nobility of soul of which we are capable has been evolved; it is the ultimate point of development in a long history of gradual creative change. That is why it is so precious, and that is why Saint-Exupéry regards the stifling of nobility as the ultimate crime, and the ignorance of it the ultimate pathos.

[1] see Albérès, *Saint-Exupéry*, pp. 91–2.

The evolutionary heritage is passed on from generation to generation, and with it the potential greatness of each man. The process is a slow one, but is sure:

> 9. La seule victoire dont je ne puis douter est celle qui loge dans le pouvoir des graines. Plantée la graine, au large des terres noires, la voilà déjà victorieuse. Mais il faut dérouler le temps pour assister à son triomphe dans le blé.   (*Pilote de Guerre*, p. 204)

The mysterious progress of evolution, always taking a step forward, fills Saint-Exupéry with admiration and wonder, and inspires some of his most eloquent passages:

> 10. Ce qui se transmettait ainsi de génération en génération, avec le lent progrès d'une croissance d'arbre, c'était la vie mais c'était aussi la conscience. Quelle mystérieuse ascension! D'une lave en fusion, d'une pâte d'étoile, d'une cellule vivante germée par miracle nous sommes issus, et, peu à peu, nous nous sommes élevés jusqu'à écrire des cantates et à peser des voies lactées. . . .
>
> La mère n'avait point seulement transmis la vie: elle avait, à ses fils, enseigné un langage, elle leur avait confié le bagage si lentement accumulé au cours des siècles, le patrimoine spirituel qu'elle avait elle-même reçu en dépôt.   (*Terre des Hommes*, p. 139)

The end-product of evolutionary progress is not always something as exalted as a Bach cantata. It can be, and usually is, the simplest thing in life, as a smile. The smile is that expression, beyond language, of an innate understanding; it is a sign of that nobility which too often lies fallow. It is an involuntary recognition of our heritage. From inanimate matter, we have evolved the smile:

> 11. un certain miracle de ce soleil qui s'était donné tant de mal, depuis tant de millions d'années pour aboutir, à travers nous, à la qualité d'un sourire qui était assez bien réussi. L'essentiel, le plus souvent, n'a point de poids. L'essential ici, en apparence, n'a été qu'un sourire.
>   (*Lettre à un Otage*, p. 41)

Hence, given the wide scope of his vision, Saint-Exupéry insists throughout his work that he is concerned with realizing the full value of the *species* man. 'Moi, j'aime l'espèce', he wrote in his notebook. It is a point to which we shall have to return in discussing Saint-Exupéry's Humanism in the following chapter.

C. Fraternity

We have seen in the chapter on *Vol de Nuit* that men can best release their latent nobility by giving themselves to the *métier* at the expense of their individual, superficial needs. In *Terre des Hommes* the emphasis is placed not so much on this rather austere, harsh view of the heroic life, but on the aspect of comradeship which derives from it. By giving oneself to the *métier* one is giving oneself to one's comrades, and thereby satisfying a far deeper need (a need which is also inherited in evolutionary terms), the need for *bonds*. A man does not merely require nourishment for the body or exercise for the muscles, he requires the sense of belonging to the 'tribe', or being part of a great concert, of knowing that he is an important part of the whole. In short, the vocational life brings with it the supreme joy of human relationships:

1. La grandeur d'un métier est, peut-être, avant tout, d'unir les hommes: il n'est qu'un luxe véritable, et c'est celui des relations humaines. (*Terre des Hommes*, p. 21)
2. Liés à nos frères par un but commun et qui se situe en dehors de nous, alors seulement nous respirons et l'expérience nous montre qu'aimer ce n'est point nous regarder l'un l'autre mais regarder ensemble dans la même direction. Il n'est de camarades que s'ils s'unissent dans la même cordée, vers le même sommet en quoi ils se retrouvent. (ibid., p. 132)
3. Plaindre, c'est encore être deux, c'est encore être divisé. Mais il existe une altitude des relations où la reconnaissance comme la pitié perdent leur sens. C'est là que l'on respire comme un prisonnier délivré. . . . Nous étions les branches d'un même arbre. (ibid., p. 131)

The community of men is not mere arithmetic. It is not the *collection* of men. It is a certain organization and structure (again, inherited), which is above all spiritual. Men united by a community of spirit and intention, each strained to support the other towards the achievement of a goal which lies beyond them all. Hence the brotherhood of men within a community implies their interdependence; they are responsible towards each other, and towards the community as a whole, whose *permanence* it is their duty to maintain. The community offers a denial in the face of the transience of life.

More than this, the members of a community are responsible to the species, to all mankind, since they are the living expression of that nobility which is mankind's greatest glory.

The perfect example of a man who, by his actions, confirms the destiny and dignity of all men, is Henri Guillaumet. Saint-Exupéry recounts the story of Guillaumet's loss in the Andes, of his superhuman efforts to survive over several days without food and almost dead from exposure, and of his miraculous rediscovery when hope had all but been lost. He had survived because he owed it to his comrades and to mankind; no other creature would have been able to summon such responsibility:

4. 'Ce que j'ai fait, je le jure, jamais aucune bête ne l'aurait fait. Cette phrase, la plus noble que je connaisse, cette phrase qui situe l'homme, qui l'honore, qui rétablit les hiérarchies vraies . . . Sa grandeur, c'est de se sentir responsable. Responsable de lui, du courrier, et des camarades qui espèrent. Il tient dans ses mains leur peine ou leur joie. Responsable de ce qui se bâtit de neuf, là-bas, chez les vivants, à quoi il doit participer. Responsable un peu du destin des hommes, dans la mesure de son travail. . . . Etre homme, c'est précisément être responsable. . . . C'est sentir, en posant sa pierre, que l'on contribue à bâtir le monde.   (ibid., pp. 30–1)

We may now discern how far Saint-Exupéry has come since the temptations of romantic love in *Courrier Sud*. Real love is not to stand opposite someone, but to stand side by side *with* someone, in unspoken but profound comradeship. Love is to recognize one's responsibility.

Saint-Exupéry never talks of carnal desire. But he does talk of bonds, of *liens*, which, without demonstrations of affection (which he detests), unite men to each other in a common purpose. One may then properly talk of 'love':

> 5. Nous n'y reconnaissons pas l'amour. L'amour auquel nous songeons d'ordinaire est d'un pathétique plus tumultueux. Mais il s'agit, ici, de l'amour véritable: un réseau de liens qui fait devenir. (*Pilote de Guerre*, p. 198)

And what else does the fox mean but love, when he asks the Little Prince to 'tame' him? Here, *apprivoiser* signifies the creation of bonds which unite two beings in friendship and responsibility:

> 6. . . . Qu'est-ce que signifie 'apprivoiser'?
> — C'est une chose trop oubliée, dit le renard. Ça signifie 'créer des liens'. . . .
> . . . Les hommes ont oublié cette vérité, dit le renard. Mais tu ne dois pas l'oublier. Tu deviens responsable pour toujours de ce que tu as apprivoisé. Tu es responsable de ta rose. (*Le Petit Prince*, pp. 68, 74)

Is not the story of the smile in *Lettre à un Otage* yet another indication of the fundamental, spiritual love/fraternity which is the very essence of humanity?

Saint-Exupéry is being interrogated by Spanish officials. Suddenly one of them offers him a cigarette, and smiles. The author is almost embarrassed at recounting the incident, as it seems so insignificant and mundane. But it only *seems* so, because it is an experience above the capacity of language; it has its roots in a bond-relationship which is as ancient as man himself, and which lies so deep as to be forgotten. Saint-Exupéry speaks once again of a 'miracle', one of the key-words to his thought, and of 'parenté':

> 7. Les hommes non plus n'avaient pas bougé, mais, alors qu'ils m'apparaissaient une seconde plus tôt comme plus

éloignés de moi qu'une espèce antédiluvienne, voici qu'ils naissaient à une vie proche. J'éprouvais une extraordinaire sensation de présence. C'est bien ça: de présence! Et je sentais ma parenté.   (*Lettre à un Otage*, p. 53)

In this respect, Saint-Exupéry seems to reflect, and sometimes anticipate, much contemporary thought in ethology. The work of Konrad Lorenz has made popular new ideas on the antiquity of human relationships. It is now widely accepted that the human community is a reflection of communities established by early primates, and is by no means an evolutionarily novel invention. The intimate collaboration of members of a primate community was an essential precondition of any achievement by the community as a whole. If the community was not bound by this profound 'fraternity', this denial of individuality, then the species sunk into extinction

Critics have more usually discerned the influence of Bergson. And there is certainly more evidence to support the contention that Saint-Exupéry's regard for the supremacy of instinct over reason is taken directly from Bergson.

The social anthropologist Claude Lévi-Strauss, writing in a totally different context but reaching conclusions which are none the less appropriate here, has said that a properly constituted humanism must place the respect for others before self-interest. His painstakingly thorough analysis of myth led him to the conclusion that one of the purposes of myth was to demonstrate that the evils of the world were caused by self-interest.

Saint-Exupéry is no organized philosopher, but he has a remarkable insight into these truths of the condition of all life, and his greatest fear is that the human species should slide into oblivion for want of acknowledging its ancient call to fraternity, and through it, achieving its permanence; he had a worrying vision of a world in which fratricidal strife, born of egotism, should herald the disintegration of the species:

8. Il faut, pour essayer de dégager cet essentiel, oublier un instant les divisions, qui, une fois admises, entrainent tout

un Coran de vérités inébranlables et le fanatisme qui en découle.   (*Terre des Hommes*, p. 134)

Those critics who reduce Saint-Exupéry's concept of brother-hood to the level of boy-scout loyalty (such as Jean Cau), or worse, identify his fraternity with base militarism, have missed the point entirely. Saint-Exupéry's thought soars to a much higher level, is concerned with a much wider horizon. He is concerned with Man, not with the petty partisan squabbles of men who disgrace the species. He deplores artificial political divisions:

9. Ce stupide patriotisme de XXe siècle n'est plus que du mauvais esprit d'équipe. Il coïncide avec l'enthousiasme d'une équipe fondée sur la seule couleur du maillot et négligeant les parentés vrais.   (*Carnets*, p. 86)

Recognition of the true brotherhood of man, *within the species*, enables men working together to achieve the full flowering of the species. It is the very antithesis of divisive camps. When the pilots join together and give of themselves for the sake of the community, they are not united *against* anything, but *for* the spiritual value of the community which they have founded:

10. Alors on s'épaule l'un l'autre. On découvre que l'on appartient à la même communauté. On s'élargit par la découverte d'autres consciences. On se regarde avec un grand sourire. On est semblable à ce prisonnier délivré qui s'émerveille de l'immensité de la mer.
                              (*Terre des Hommes*, p. 23)
11. L'homme n'est qu'un noeud de relations. Les relations comptent seules pour l'homme.
                              (*Pilote de Guerre*, p. 171)

In creating and serving a community, Saint-Exupéry and his pilots are creating Man:

12. L'Homme commune mesure des camarades.
                              (ibid., p. 217)

D. Men Without Bonds

Deprived of the ties of fraternity which are their natural and rightful inheritance, men will flounder in a hopeless void. Such is the case of Bark, the Arab slave to whom Saint-Exupéry gives his liberty:

> 1. Mais cette liberté lui parut amère: elle lui découvrait surtout à quel point il lui manquait de liens avec le monde. . . .
> . . . Alors qu'il éprouvait, comme on éprouve une faim profonde, le besoin d'être un homme parmi les hommes, lié aux hommes.   (*Terre des Hommes*, pp. 79–80)

Bark has only 'la liberté de n'être point'. (*Pilote de Guerre*, p. 184) Similarly, Saint-Exupéry himself, called upon in wartime to burn villages and systematically destroy the very ties with mankind which he so values, experiences the anguish of isolation:

> 2. Il est difficile d'exister. L'homme n'est qu'un noeud de relations, et voilà que mes liens ne valent plus grand-chose.
> (*Pilote de Guerre*, p. 99)

The man who breaks his ties with his fellows, destroys himself. For no one has need of him any longer, and he only exists in so far as he knows what he is not. He has nothing to offer, there is no one who requires anything of him. He is no longer part of the community of men. His liberty is therefore totally negative and illusory.

Writing of the Frenchmen who fled their country during the war, in order to protect their investments in foreign banks, Saint-Exupéry observes that they are listless, floating, lacking in any responsibility, because they have severed the ties which alone gave density to their lives. It is the nearest Saint-Exupéry comes to pity, an emotion rare in his work:

> 3. Ce n'est point d'argent qu'ils manquaient, mais de densité. Ils n'étaient plus l'homme de telle maison, de tel ami, de telle responsabilité. Ils jouaient le rôle, mais ce

n'était plus vrai. Personne n'avait besoin d'eux, personne ne s'apprêtait à faire appel à eux. . . . Certes, mes reve-nants, personne ne les haïssait, personne ne les jalousait, personne ne les importunait. Mais personne ne les aimait du seul amour qui comptât. (*Lettre à un Otage*, p. 21)

A man without ties is a man in disarray. He is weightless, disoriented. The most bustling town is a chaotic sea of inde-pendent ghosts, if it contains no community united in the creation of Man:

4. Car le désert n'est pas là où l'on croit. Le Sahara est plus vivant qu'une capitale et la ville la plus grouillante se vide si les pôles essentiels de la vie sont désaimantés.
                                                              (ibid., p. 32)
5. Les hommes? Il en existe, je crois, six ou sept. Je les ai aperçu il y a des années. Mais on ne sait jamais où les trouver. Le vent les promène. Ils manquent de racines, ça les gêne beaucoup. . . .
   . . . ils ne savent plus ce qu'ils cherchent. Alors ils s'agitent et tournent en rond.   (*Le Petit Prince*, pp. 62, 80)

E. Un Sens A La Vie

One of the dominant ideas of *Terre des Hommes* is Saint-Exupéry's ardent desire to show men that life can have a mean-ing if only they will give it one. All his life he was tormented by men's apparent neglect of their innate qualities; nothing upset him more than to observe men in ignorance of their potential. When Pierre Bost wrote in *Le Figaro Littéraire* of 9 July 1964 that Saint-Exupéry sought for the meaning of life without ever finding it, he was not entirely accurate. For Saint-Exupéry maintained that the meaning of life was within the grasp of all of us, if only we would look into ourselves. It was evident in our instinctive need for *plénitude* or *épanouisse-ment*:

1. Il est deux cent millions d'hommes, en Europe, qui n'ont point de sens et voudraient naître. L'industrie les a arrachés au langage des lignées paysannes et les a enfermés

C

dans ces ghettos énormes qui ressemblent à des gares de triage encombrées de rames de wagons noirs. Du fond des cités ouvrières, ils voudraient être réveillés. . . . On a cru que pour les grandir il suffisait de les vêtir, de les nourrir, de répondre à tous leurs besoins.

(*Terre des Hommes*, p. 135)

2. Comment favoriser en nous cette sorte de délivrance? Tout est paradoxale en l'homme, on le sait bien. On assure le pain à celui-là pour lui permettre de créer, et il s'endort, le conquérant victorieux s'amollit, le généreux, si on l'enrichit, devient ladre.   (ibid., p. 123)

Saint-Exupéry asks not that we should admire the men who have achieved self-fulfilment, men such as Guillaumet and Mermoz. Indeed, he deplores such admiration (as did Rivière in *Vol de Nuit*). He asks only that we should recognize the value of the vocational life, as a deliverance from mediocrity, and that we should embrace it ourselves in order to release the greatness which lies concealed within us. In so doing, we should do no more than obey the most fundamental instinct. Man's desire is not for happiness, he says, but for 'plénitude'.

In a long passage, which again recalls Konrad Lorenz, Saint-Exupéry describes the migratory flight of farmyard ducks, who suddenly reveal themselves to be other than they appeared. He relates also his own taming of gazelles at Cap Juby, and their sudden inexplicable desire to escape back to the desert whence they came, as if attracted by some irresistible magnet. Why do they want to leave? Why *must* they leave? They do not know. They have lived in captivity since birth, have never seen the desert, yet they are impelled by a strange, imperious instinct to move:

3. Ce qu'elles cherchent, vous le savez, c'est l'étendue qui les accomplira. Elles veulent devenir gazelles et danser leur danse. . . . Peu importent les chacals, si la vérité des gazelles est de goûter la peur, qui les contraint seul à se surpasser et tire d'elles les plus hautes vertiges. Qu'importe le lion si la vérité des gazelles est d'être ouvertes d'un coup de griffe dans le soleil. Vous les regardez et vous songez; les voilà prises de nostalgie. La nostalgie, c'est le désir

d'on ne sait quoi . . . Il existe, l'objet du désir, mais il n'est point de mots pour le dire.
Et à nous, que nous manque-t-il? (ibid., p. 131)

When Saint-Exupéry talks here of nostalgia, he is referring to that peculiar impulsion of the species, which is more mysterious even than instinct (since instinct is often learnt), and he avers that men too possess a nostalgia of the species which is the only possible explanation for their need to 'get up and go', to *do* something, to accede to that indescribable inner command – 'cette plénitude qui me gonfle si fort'. (*Pilote de Guerre*, p. 186)

The need for *plénitude* can be satisfied, as we have seen, by embracing a life of self-abnegation, giving of oneself for one's fellows in a community dedicated to the advancement of the species.

But it is not easy. And Saint-Exupéry not once suggests that it is. One must first learn to reject the material values which cushion man against an awareness of his own greatness.

Materialism is the death of the species.

F. L'Homme Abimé

Saint-Exupéry's purpose is to awaken the unknown and unsuspected man hidden beneath the well-clothed comfort of the bureaucrat. He wants to take the bureaucrat by the shoulders and shake him. His attitude towards such men is a mixture of contempt for the materialism which stifles them, and compassion for the victim of that materialism:

1. Vieux bureaucrate, mon camarade ici présent, nul jamais ne t'a fait évader et tu n'en es point responsable. Tu as construit ta paix à force d'aveugler de ciment, comme le font les termites, toutes les échappées vers la lumière. Tu t'es roulé en boule dans ta sécurité bourgeoise, tes routines, tes rites étouffants de ta vie provinciale . . . tu ne te poses point de questions sans réponse: tu es un petit bourgeois

de Toulouse. Nul ne t'a saisi par les épaules quand il en
était temps encore. Maintenant, la glaise dont tu es formé
a séché, et s'est durcie, et nul en toi ne saurait désormais
réveiller le musicien endormi, ou le poète, ou l'astronome
qui peut-être t'habitaient d'abord.

(*Terre des Hommes*, p. 10)

The passage recalls Herlin in *Courrier Sud*, and Robineau in
Vol de Nuit, both men whose lives are stagnant through inactivity; it also recalls Rivière's impatience with the 'petits
bourgeois autour de leur kiosque à musique'. Their tragedy is
that they are blind to their potential:

2. Je ne comprends plus ces populations des trains de
   banlieue, ces hommes qui se croient des hommes, et qui
   cependant sont réduits, par une pression qu'ils ne sentent
   pas, comme les fourmis, à l'usage qui en est fait. De quoi
   remplissent-ils, quand ils sont libres, leurs absurdes petits
   dimanches?
   . . . Je n'aime pas que l'on abîme les hommes.

(ibid., p. 116)

How is the tragedy possible? Because modern urban civilization has lost touch with the forces of nature, which are man's
rightful décor, and has reduced men to a mere collectivity.
Often does Saint-Exupéry refer to men in industrial cities as
'mice' or 'insects', piled one upon another, without room to
spread their wings. No wonder their lives are empty:

3. Il est, en cet insecte muré avec sa provision de nourriture,
   quelque chose qui n'est point de l'homme. L'homme doit
   chercher ailleurs et s'évader (musique, poème, religion,
   sacrifice, universalité, etc.): le petit ingénieur de l'X avec
   lequel je déjeunais à Perpignan et qui ne savait rien hors
   les équations de sa fonction et le poker d'as: quelque
   chose en lui est manqué.
   Il peut s'imaginer heureux, il peut se préférer ainsi, il
   manque le bonheur véritable (au titre où, n'étant plus un
   but, il n'est que le sentiment de richesse) qui accompagne
   une activité véritablement humaine, il ne sait point le goût
   de la pleine mer.   (*Carnets*, p. 41)

Bridge-players, golfers, pen-pushers, the entire army of town-dwellers in slavery to their material comfort and their professional advancement, they are all deceived, and, pathetically, they are content to remain so. The Little Prince met one such on each planet that he visited – the narcissist who was happy only when being admired, the king who enjoyed being obeyed, the businessman who consumed all his time and interest in counting his money, so much so that he did not even hear the little prince's questions, and one in particular, who was proud of his importance. Saint-Exupéry's anger cries out in this passage:

4. Je connais une planète où il y a un monsieur cramoisi. Il n'a jamais respiré une fleur. Il n'a jamais regardé une étoile. Il n'a jamais aimé personne. Il n'a jamais rien fait d'autre que des additions. Et toute la journée il répète comme toi: 'Je suis un homme sérieux! Je suis un homme sérieux!' et ça le fait gonfler d'orgueil. Mais ce n'est pas un homme, c'est un champignon!

(*Le Petit Prince*, p. 29)

The mistake is to assume that material comfort can contribute anything to the happiness of men. Saint-Exupéry sets no store whatever by the gathering of possessions. In his last work, when the despair born of the war and his own inability to convey his message to men had soured him, his compassion for the petits bourgeois turned to contempt, and his message was shouted rather than stated with the calm eloquence of *Terre des Hommes*:

5. Ainsi n'eurent-ils plus à s'inquiéter pour leur subsistance et chacun eût pu dire: 'Peu m'importe ce qui ne me concerne point. Si j'ai mon thé, mon sucre et mon âne bien nourri et ma femme à côté de moi, si mes enfants progressent en âge et en vertu — alors je suis pleinement heureux et je ne demande rien d'autre . . .'
Mais qui eût pu les croire heureux? Nous allions parfois les visiter quand mon père désirait m'enseigner. 'Vois, disait-il, ils deviennent bétail et commencent doucement de pourrir . . . non dans leur chair mais dans leur coeur.'

(*Citadelle*, p. 549)

From regarding materialism as a lamentable deviation from the truth, Saint-Exupéry now considers it to be a positive evil, a disgusting aberration, the most dangerous enemy of man's profound need for fulfilment:

> 6. 'Si tu veux qu'ils soient frères, oblige-les à bâtir une tour. Mais si tu veux qu'ils se haïssent, jette-leur du grain . . .'
> (ibid., p. 541)
> 7. Car une civilisation repose sur ce qui est exigé des hommes, non sur ce qui leur est fourni.   (ibid.)

The evil is nurtured and propagated by that monster of the twentieth century – the publicity machine. For Saint-Exupéry (who was himself once employed as a travelling salesman), the principle of sales promotion engenders the ultimate degradation of man – apathy:

> 8. Une industrie basée sur le profit tend à créer — par l'éducation — des hommes pour le chewing-gum et non du chewing-gum pour les hommes. Ainsi de la nécessité pour l'automobile de créer la valeur *automobile* est né le stupide petit gigolo de 1926 exclusivement animé dans les bars par des images et comparaisons de carrosseries. Ainsi, du film, est née, dans la pâte humaine la plus admirable du monde, la star vide et stupide entre les stupides. Cet animal creux, et dont je ne crois même point qu'elle s'ennuie, car elle n'est pas née encore.
> (*Carnets*, p. 29)

The closing pages of *Terre des Hommes* are an eloquent expression of Saint-Exupéry's faith that men might still be rescued from the baseness of twentieth-century life, which suffocates their natural nobility and turns them into obedient puppets. He starts by addressing the bureaucrats who appear like other men, like the pilots, but are nevertheless unaware that their lives are lacking, 'ils ne connaissaient point qu'ils avaient faim'.

Why is it that, out of such fine material ('la pâte humaine'), such mediocrity should be produced? What has gone wrong? Even an animal preserves its natural grace into old age, but a man, once his natural nobility has been snuffed out, is a poor,

miserable, despicable creature. Saint-Exupéry suffers to see
man thus degraded:

> 9. Le mystère, c'est qu'ils soient devenus ces paquets de
> glaise. Dans quel moule terrible ont-ils passé, marqués
> par lui comme par une machine à emboutir? Un animal
> vieilli conserve sa grâce. Pourquoi cette belle argile
> humaine est-elle abîmée? (*Terre des Hommes*, p. 141)

His suffering is not derived from pity for the individual who
is so debased; Saint-Exupéry is not concerned with individuals.
What causes him anguish is that so many possibilities of greatness are smothered at birth, or trampled into an early confor-
mity. So many 'belles promesses de la vie' are destined never
to be fulfilled. Were Mozart to live now, would he too not be
forced into mediocrity? And in killing Mozart, are we not
killing the greatness of the human species?

> 10. Quand il naît par mutation dans les jardins une rose
> nouvelle, voilà tous les jardiniers qui s'émeuvent. On
> isole la rose, on cultive la rose, on la favorise. Mais il
> n'est point de jardinier pour les hommes. Mozart enfant
> sera marqué comme les autres par la machine à emboutir.
> Mozart fera ses plus hautes joies de musique pourrie,
> dans la puanteur des cafés-concerts. Mozart est con-
> damné.
> 11. C'est quelque chose comme l'espèce humaine et non
> l'individu qui est blessé ici, qui est lésé. Je ne crois guère
> à la pitié. Ce qui me tourmente, c'est le point de vue du
> jardinier. Ce qui me tourmente, ce n'est point cette
> misère, dans laquelle, après tout, on s'installe aussi bien
> que dans la paresse. Des générations d'orientaux vivent
> dans la crasse et s'y plaisent. Ce qui me tourmente, les
> soupes populaires ne le guérissent point. Ce qui me
> tourmente, ce ne sont ni ces creux, ni ces bosses, ni cette
> laideur. C'est un peu, dans chacun des ces hommes,
> Mozart assassiné. (ibid., p. 142)

These, almost the last words of the book, are tinged with a
note of sadness, even despair. Saint-Exupéry then added a
final sentence (against, apparently, the advice of his friends),

which re-asserted his faith, and changed the feeling with
which the book must leave the reader:

Seul l'Esprit, s'il souffle sur la glaise, peut créer l'Homme.

In his next book, *Pilote de Guerre*, Saint-Exupéry was to
develop this Humanism, and clarify what he meant by *l'Esprit*.

But we are justified, at this point, in neglecting chronology
for a moment, to consider a letter written by Saint-Exupéry
shortly before his death, and published in the *Figaro Littéraire*
four years later. It resumes the theme of *l'homme abîmé* or
Mozart assassiné which had formed such a large part of *Terre
des Hommes*, but the author no longer insists on adding a final
message of hope:

12. Aujourd'hui, je suis profondément triste, et en profon-
deur. Je suis triste pour ma génération qui est vide de
toute substance humaine ... Aujourd'hui que nous
sommes plus désséchés que des briques, nous sourions
de ces niaiseries ... les hommes refusent d'être réveillés
à une vie spirituelle quelconque. Ils font honnêtement
une sorte de travail à la chaîne. Siècle de la publicité, du
système Bedeau, des régimes totalitaires, des armées
sans clairons ni drapeaux, ni messe pour les morts. Je
hais mon époque de toutes mes forces. L'homme y meurt
de soif.

Ah! Général, il n'y a qu'un problème, un seul de par
le monde. Rendre aux hommes une signification spirituelle, des inquiétudes spirituelles ... on ne peut plus
vivre de frigidaires, de politique, de bilans et de mots
croisés, voyez-vous. On ne peut plus. On ne peut plus
vivre sans poésie, couleur, ni amour. ...

... Nous sommes étonnamment bien châtrés. Ainsi som-
mes-nous enfin libres. On nous a coupé les bras et les
jambes, puis on nous a laissés libres de marcher. Mais
je hais cette époque où l'homme devient, sous un totali-
tarisme universel, bétail doux, poli, et tranquille. ...

... l'homme châtré de tout son pouvoir créateur et qui
ne sait même plus, du fond de son village, créer une
danse ni une chanson. L'homme qu'on alimente en culture de confection, en culture standard, comme on alimente les boeufs en foin. C'est cela, l'homme d'aujourd'-
hui.   (*Lettre au Général X*)

In an even later letter, addressed to Pierre Dalloz, and not received by him until one week after Saint-Exupéry's death, the message of despair is yet more clear. These are Saint-Exupéry's last known words; if I am killed, he writes, I shall regret absolutely nothing:

> 13. Si je suis descendu, je ne regretterai absolument rien.
> La termitière future m'épouvante et je hais leur vertu
> de robots. Moi, j'étais fait pour être jardinier.
> (quoted in *Pierre Chevrier*, p. 189)

G. Death

Readers of these last letters of Saint-Exupéry have sometimes concluded that he sought his own death. To suggest such is to falsify the man's entire life and work.

Certainly, he was not afraid of death, he did not feel 'cette angoisse devant la mort dont on nous rebat les oreilles'. (*Terre des Hommes*, p. 99) But were he to seek death, or willingly to accede to its call, he would sin against the very values of comradeship and responsibility towards his fellows and mankind which he so fervently proclaimed. Only such responsibility kept Guillaumet alive in the Andes, and inspired Saint-Exupéry's own will to live when lost in the desert.

At the same time, he refuses to see anything tragic in death itself. As the Little Prince says, 'J'aurai l'air d'être mort et ce ne sera pas vrai.' (*Le Petit Prince*, p. 89)

Death need not be regarded as the 'end' of something, if one has led a life which has contributed to the creation of Man; if one has given a meaning to life, then death is by no means a negation of that meaning:

> 1. Quand nous prendrons conscience de notre rôle, même
> le plus effacé, alors seulement nous serons heureux. Alors
> seulement nous pourrons vivre en paix et mourir en paix,
> car ce qui donne un sens à la vie donne un sens à la mort.
> (*Terre des Hommes*, p. 138)

There are many pages in Saint-Exupéry's work where he

talks of the passage of generations, of the great inheritance of mankind which continues and survives individual death, and which sees death as a step forward in the huge story of Man. As a plant dies, scatters its seed, and carries forward its essence, so:

> 2. On ne meurt qu'à demi dans une lignée paysanne. Chaque existence craque à son tour comme une cosse et livre ses graines.   (*Un Sens à la Vie*, p. 181)

Death is to be accepted in the natural order of things. A life which involves the constant presence of death serves to remind one of what little importance is the passage of an individual; it is his life which matters, not his death:

> 3. J'accepte la mort. Ce n'est pas le risque que j'accepte. Ce n'est pas le combat que j'accepte. C'est la mort. J'ai appris une grande vérité. La guerre, ce n'est pas l'acceptation du risque. Ce n'est pas l'acceptation du combat. C'est, à certaines heures, pour le combattant, l'acceptation pure et simple de la mort.   (*Pilote de Guerre*, p. 143)

For the same reasons, it is wrong to lament a dead friend, in the sense that one cherishes his belongings and attempts to create the illusion that he 'lives on' in some way. The acceptance of death can create something far greater than this pathetic, evasive shadow of life. Saint-Exupéry is not a man touched by pathos; he would rather the positive presence of a dead friend, than the negative memory of a live one:

> 4. Des morts on doit faire des morts. Alors ils retrouvent, dans leur rôle de morts, une autre forme de présence.
>   (*Lettre à un Otage*, p. 12)

This attitude towards death raises the whole matter of courage in Saint-Exupéry's work. His frequent denial that he has any taste for risk *for its own sake*, as in the passage from *Pilote de Guerre* above, has not prevented his detractors from diminishing the scope of his thought. 'He goes up in his aeroplane and discovers a new form of aristocratic adventurism,' writes John Weightman (*The Observer*, 10 January 1971), 'he really wants to risk his neck for the fun of it and because the death-risk is the ultimate test of character.'

The courage of Saint-Exupéry does not reside in a lofty contempt for death, or in the taste for danger. It lies in the responsibility which accrues from an action taken *in spite of* oneself, for the affirmation of the essential fraternity of men. A courage which is not inspired with this purpose is empty vainglory:

5. Mais je me moque bien du mépris de la mort. S'il ne tire pas ses racines d'une responsabilité acceptée, il n'est que signe de pauvreté ou d'excès de jeunesse.

(Terre des Hommes, p. 31)

6. Si on lui parlait de son courage, Guillaumet hausserait les épaules. Mais on le trahirait aussi en célébrant sa modestie. Il se situe bien au-delà de cette qualité médiocre.

(ibid.)

7. Et il ne s'agit pas de vivre dangereusement. Cette formule est prétentieuse. Les toréadors ne me plaisent guère. Ce n'est pas le danger que j'aime. Je sais ce que j'aime. C'est la vie. (ibid., p. 116)

André Gide, in his preface to *Vol de Nuit*, quotes a letter from Saint-Exupéry in which the author condemns mere courage as a sign of self-indulgence:

8. Ce n'est pas fait de bien beaux sentiments: un peu de rage, un peu de vanité, beaucoup d'entêtement et un plaisir sportif vulgaire. Surtout l'exaltation de sa force physique, qui pourtant n'a rien à y voir. . . . Jamais plus je n'admirerai un homme qui ne serait que courageux.

(Vol de Nuit, p. 3)

For this reason Rivière discourages would-be admirers; they do not understand that he and his pilots are creating something which goes far beyond ostentatious courage:

9. Rivière craignait certains admirateurs. Ils ne comprenaient pas le caractère sacré de l'aventure, et leurs exclamations en faussaient le sens, diminuaient l'homme.

(ibid., p. 15)

If there is courage, it is to be found in the *will* to act, to throw off the yoke of personal vanity and ambition, and release the inner man who will accept his responsibility, through his acts, for the essence of mankind. As André Rousseaux has written (in *Le Figaro Littéraire*, 25 April 1939):

> Ce qui compte, ce n'est pas le mépris de la mort, c'est ce qui va naître.

Should you tell Mermoz (as John Weightman does) that it is not worth risking his life to carry a packet of envelopes across the Andes, he would laugh: 'La Vérité, c'est l'homme qui naissait en lui quand il passait les Andes.'

> La vérité pour l'homme, c'est ce qui fait de lui un homme .

5

Pilote de Guerre

Published in 1942, after the author's first experiences as a reconnaissance pilot, *Pilote de Guerre* is a meditation on the folly and disgrace of war. It starts as a personal record of Saint-Exupéry's own passionate reactions to the disaster of his country's defeat and humiliation, and as such, it was the first book on the subject to reveal the French spirit to the world.

Saint-Exupéry sees the disaster of France as part of a much deeper crisis – the loss of a spiritual unitive force in the world. Man has neglected the life of the spirit in favour of the life of the intellect.

Men must learn to subordinate reason and logic to the superior claims of the spiritual life. The intelligence cannot, of its nature, grasp the meaning and purpose of life; it can only create confusion and enmity. Man must govern his acts by the spirit alone.

The subject of the spirit allows Saint-Exupéry to restate themes which have occupied the greater part of his earlier work; the life of the spirit discloses a sense of *mutual brotherhood* and of *sacrifice* to the community; the spirit teaches *responsibility* of men to subordinate themselves to the supreme value, which is Man.

In the Middle Ages men had a common focus in God, which gave them a moral incentive to strive beyond their utilitarian urges and desires. They had an intuitive, mystical, unifying vision of life. Modern man has developed his faculties of analysis at the expense of his spiritual perceptions, and has thus lost this cohesion. Without returning to Christianity we must recognize the worth of the spiritual inheritance we have been left.

The book ends with an impassioned Humanist *credo* which reveals the nature of the civilization he and his comrades are struggling to defend, and replaces the religion of God with the religion of Man.

A. War

With incredible injustice, Jean Cau has written that Saint-Exupéry's work is dedicated to the celebration of a military ethic. It is difficult to imagine a more false reading of his books.

Saint-Exupéry was never an advocate of militarism. He was acutely conscious of the danger that a military life might seduce men into believing that therein lay the answer to their need for fulfilment. Towards the end of *Terre des Hommes*, written before the war, but during the period of gathering menace in Europe, he specifically condemned the blind intoxication of nationalism. Simple patriotism does nothing to enhance the nobility of man; on the contrary, it redirects the forces of conformism:

> 1. Tous, plus ou moins confusément, éprouvent le besoin de naître. Mais il est des solutions qui trompent. Certes on peut animer les hommes, en les habillant d'uniformes. . . . On peut enivrer les Allemands de l'ivresse d'être Allemands et compatriotes de Beethoven. On peut en saouler jusqu'au soutier. C'est, certes, plus facile que de tirer du soutier un Beethoven.   (*Terre des Hommes*, p. 136)

When he came to live through the senselessness of war himself, Saint-Exupéry wrote with the anger of one who feels that the human race has suffered a grotesque insult. He joined in the game without the support of any conviction that he was fighting *for* something: 'nous jouons aux gendarmes et aux voleurs'. Soldiers burning villages, looting, killing, adding to chaos and disorder, without any faith or exaltation. Why? Because, like the emigrants described in *Lettre à un Otage*, they have been torn from their bonds; they are being forced to act against nature, to destroy those very ties with mankind which, in the roots of their being, they most long for. In short, their acts are gratuitous, robbed of all meaning:

  2. Arrachés à leur cadre, à leur travail, à leurs devoirs, ils ont perdu toute signification. . . . Pour que les actes soient fervents, il faut que leur signification apparaisse. (*Pilote de Guerre*, pp. 124, 94)
  3. L'homme n'est qu'un noeud de relations, et voilà que mes liens ne valent plus grand-chose. (ibid., p. 99)

Instead of creating bonds, war severs them. Instead of glorifying man by an act of responsibility, war degrades him:

  4. si nous sommes de ceux qui reviennent, nous n'aurons rien à raconter. J'ai autrefois vécu des aventures: la création des lignes postales, la dissidence saharienne, l'Amérique du Sud, mais la guerre n'est point une aventure. L'aventure repose sur la richesse des liens qu'elle établit, des problèmes qu'elle pose, des créations qu'elle provoque. Il ne suffit pas, pour transformer en aventure le simple jeu de pile ou face, d'engager sur lui la vie et la mort. La guerre n'est pas une aventure. La guerre est une maladie. Comme le typhus. (ibid., p. 76)

Most of all, and most obviously, war is anti-human, 'monstrueusement en dehors de l'humain'. (p. 123) Its only value is a negative one: to teach man to beware the arguments of insidious reason and logic which can so deflect mankind from its true course of development.

B. The Inadequacy of Intelligence

Saint-Exupéry, the writer whose life is in his work, is not a man with a theory to be proven. Indeed, he is profoundly anti-intellectual. The experience of the war confirmed his deep distrust of ideas which divide and confuse men. He dreams of a civilization 'où l'homme est respecté au-delà de ses idées'. (*Carnets*, p. 86) He suspects the intelligence of pure intellectuals, for 'les démarches de la raison sont incertaines'. (*Lettre à un Otage*, p. 63) Intelligence is sterile; truth is not to be demonstrated, *cannot* be demonstrated; it must be intuited:

1. Connaître, ce n'est point démonter, ni expliquer. C'est accéder à la vision.   (*Pilote de Guerre*, p. 54)

Logic, reason, discussion, all the common games of the intelligence, are capable of proving anything. But the proofs they offer are deceptive; they have nothing to do with life, only with the rules of their own game:

2. La vérité, ce n'est pas ce qui se démontre. . . . Si cette religion, si cette culture, si cette échelle de valeurs, si cette forme d'activité et non telles autres, favorisent dans l'homme cette plénitude, délivrent en lui un grand seigneur qui s'ignorait, c'est que cette échelle de valeurs, cette culture, cette forme d'activité, sont la vérité de l'homme. La logique? Qu'elle se débrouille pour rendre compte de la vie.   (*Terre des Hommes*, p. 124)

Life is a collection of contradictions. The fanatic who believes that his system is right against all others is a victim of deception by the intelligence. It is reason, paradoxically, that breeds fanaticism, by its refusal to allow contradiction. With so many logical arguments supporting so many different truths, chaos is sewn in the world. Another paradox: chaos is the result of an exaggerated respect for coherence. It is wasted effort, for logic cannot possibly discover the essence of life:

3. Mais comme ils ne comprenaient toujours pas:
   — La logique des événements . . .
   C'est alors que mon père les insulta dans sa colère:
   — Imbéciles! leur dit-il. Bétail châtré!
   Historiens, logiciens, et critiques, vous êtes la vermine des morts et jamais ne saisirez rien de la vie.
                                           (*Citadelle*, p. 857)

Language, the expression of the intelligence, is an inadequate means of communication. It is a source of misunderstanding. While attempting to unravel contradictions, language per-

petuates them, for, like logic, language can demonstrate anything, yet feel nothing intuitively:

4. Les mots sont contradictoires? Je me moque des mots.
   (*Pilote de Guerre*, p. 204)
5. Aucune explication verbale ne remplace jamais la contemplation. L'unité de l'Etre n'est pas transportable par
   les mots. (ibid., p. 230)
6. Et je n'ai point peur de me contredire, sachant que les
   contradictions ne sont que balbutiements d'un langage
   qui ne peut encore saisir son objet. Quiconque craint la
   contradiction et demeure logique tue en lui la vie.
   (*Carnets*, p. 133)
7. les langages charrient des contradictions tellement inextri-
   cables qu'elles font désespérer du salut de l'homme.
   (*Un Sens à la Vie*, p. 155)

It is, of course, language which is the root cause of war,
since its scope is too narrow to allow of transcendental truth
above the divisions artificially created by political or intellectual exclusivity. Talking of the war, Saint-Exupéry wrote in
his notebook, 'ce sont les *mots* qui ont opéré la catastrophe'.
(p. 97)

War would not occur, had language, in its clumsiness, not
obscured the truth uniting all men:

8. Et voici qu'à nous diviser sur les méthodes, nous risquons
   de ne plus reconnaître que nous nous hâtons vers le même
   but. (*Lettre à un Otage*, p. 61)

Intelligence, then, left to germinate freely, is a dangerous and
destructive force. It neglects what Saint-Exupéry calls the
'substance' of man. It is dry, arid, stagnant. It cannot explain
the fundamental creativity of man, which defies logic, flies in
the face of reason, exists on a level beyond anything which
intellectual inquiry can comprehend. Life is the exception to
the rule, the mistake in the calculations:

9. Nous nous sommes trompés trop longtemps sur le rôle
   de l'intelligence. Nous avons négligé la substance de
   l'homme. (*Pilote de Guerre*, p. 205)

D

10. Il est une vérité plus haute que les éconcés de l'intelli-
    gence . . . il est des vérités qui sont évidentes bien
    qu'informulables.   (ibid., p. 145)
11. Créer, c'est manquer peut-être ce pas dans la danse. C'est
    donner de travers ce coup de ciseaux dans la pierre.
                                        (*Citadelle*, p. 542)
12. O prisonniers, comprenez-moi! Je vous délivre de votre
    science, de vos formules, de vos lois, de cet esclavage de
    l'esprit, de ce déterminisme plus dur que la fatalité. Je
    suis le défaut dans l'armure. Je suis la lucarne dans la
    prison. Je suis l'erreur dans le calcul: je suis la vie.
                                      (*Courrier Sud*, p. 132)

To understand life, as the Little Prince does, we must discard
the intelligence, and listen to the spirit 'qui souffle sur la
glaise', the spirit which does not explain, but inspires.

C. L'Esprit

In constant opposition to the life of the intelligence, which is
inadequate and misleading, Saint-Exupéry expounds the virtues
of the spirit, which, above all else, is a *unifying* influence;
the intelligence regards the particular, but the spirit reveals the
universal; the intelligence spreads divisions, the spirit discloses
synthesis.

1. Et la vie de l'esprit commence là où un être 'un' est conçu
   au-dessus des matériaux qui le composent.
                                   (*Lettre au Général X*)
2. Mais l'Esprit ne considère point les objets, il considère le
   sens qui les noue entre eux . . .
   . . . ça ruine la vie de l'Esprit, la logique pure.
                                 (*Pilote de Guerre*, p. 28)
3. Etre tenté, c'est être tenté, quand l'Esprit dort, de céder
   aux raisons de l'Intelligence.   (ibid., p. 52)
4. car l'esprit seul fertilise l'intelligence.   (ibid., p. 207)

The life of the spirit is variously described as 'substance',
'instinct', 'inner fulfilment', even 'poetry', and it manifests
itself in love, responsibility, loyalty, self-abnegation, or simply
a smile.

The spirit in man must be set free, mobilized, given room to breathe, since it is only the spirit which can lift man to the stars, and make him surpass himself. The spirit inhabits the stranger within each man, a stranger that is nothing more than himself converted into his own potential greatness. While the spirit lies dormant, the man is held by the ankles in his mediocrity. We must 'rendre aux hommes une signification spirituelle'.

Civilization is the work of the spirit surpassing and transcending the intelligence. And the pain of Saint-Exupéry in 1942 is to observe the civilization of Europe threatened by a loss of spiritual values:

> 5. Il me semble désormais entrevoir mieux ce qu'est une civilisation. Une civilisation est un héritage de croyances, de coutumes et de connaissances, lentement acquises au cours des siècles, difficiles parfois à justifier par la logique, mais qui se justifient d'elles-mêmes, comme des chemins, s'ils conduisent quelque part, puisqu'elles ouvrent à l'homme son étendue intérieure.
> . . . car l'étendue est pour l'esprit, non pour les yeux.
> (ibid., pp. 105–106)
> 6. une politique n'a de sens qu'à condition d'être au service d'une évidence spirituelle. (*Lettre à un Otage*, p. 62)

Civilization is not, therefore, a system imposed from without, but an inward presence, independent of external circumstances. Man carries his spiritual heritage with him wherever he treads. Even in the desert, where there is no tangible evidence of a superior value, man is still governed by the spirit:

> 7. l'homme est animé d'abord par des sollicitations invisibles. L'homme est gouverné par l'Esprit. Je vaux, dans le désert, ce que valent mes divinités. (ibid., p. 29)

In *Terre des Hommes*, Saint-Exupéry relates how he and other pilots, marooned for a while in the desert, founded their own spontaneous civilization, composed of no more (though it is much!) than the spirituality which united them to each other. And, observing the young girls and old women in the public square of Punta Arenas, the southernmost town in the

world, he reflects upon the tenacity of man who can build his
spiritual edifice on the insecure foundations of a thoroughly
inhospitable land.

By implication, the body holds no importance; it is the mere
outer shell. The life of the spirit teaches one contempt for
bodily comfort:

8. On s'est tant occupé de son corps. On l'a tellement
   habillé, lavé, soigné, rasé, abreuvé, nourri. On s'est
   identifié à cet animal domestique. On l'a conduit chez le
   tailleur, chez le médecin, chez le chirurgien. On a souffert
   avec lui. On a crié avec lui. On a aimé avec lui. On dit de
   lui: c'est moi. Et voilà tout à coup que cette illusion
   s'éboule. On se moque bien du corps. On le relègue au
   rang de valetaille.   (*Pilote de Guerre*, p. 167)
9. Le corps alors n'est plus qu'un bon outil, le corps n'est
   plus qu'un serviteur.   (*Terre des Hommes*, p. 30)

Had the body been a consideration of any importance, then
Saint-Exupéry and Prévot would most certainly have died in
the Libyan desert, where for three days, in paralysing heat,
they were without water. The body demanded nourishment,
but the invisible power of the spirit ensured endurance and
ultimate survival. The same was true of Guillaumet, abandoned
to thirty degrees of frost for a whole week in the Andes, without sustenance of any kind. As we have seen in *Terre des
Hommes*, the spirit manifested itself in an overwhelming
sense of responsibility, to one's friends, and to mankind. Without it, both Saint-Exupéry and Guillaumet would have willingly surrendered to the peace of death. Guillaumet recounted
that it took every ounce of his spiritual strength not to sink
into the welcoming cushion of snow and end his agony. Saint-
Exupéry also, on another occasion when his aircraft crashed
into the sea, and his cockpit rapidly filled with water, felt the
soothing solace of oblivion creep over him. He did not panic,
he did not answer the call of self-preservation; he eventually
escaped in answer to the call of responsibility.

It is yet another paradox in Saint-Exupéry's thought that

the ultimate manifestation of the spirit is *self-sacrifice*, not in death, for that would be mere bravado, but in continuing to live when the opportunity of death is irresistible. Sacrifice is the triumph of the spirit over the body, the gift of oneself in despite of self-interest.

D. Sacrifice

Sacrifice begins with an acknowledgement of one's responsibility to all men:

1. Moi, dit mon père, je suis responsable de tous les actes de tous les hommes. (*Citadelle*, p. 855)
2. Chacun est responsable de tous. Chacun est seul responsable. Chacun est seul responsable de tous. Je comprends pour la première fois l'un des mystères de la religion dont est sortie la civilisation que je revendique comme mienne: 'Porter les péchés des hommes. . . .' Et chacun porte tous les péchés de tous les hommes
(*Pilote de Guerre*, p. 212)

This is the first time in the whole of Saint-Exupéry's work that the word 'sin' has occurred, and it would be entirely misleading to lend it the obvious Christian interpretation. The author means, by this analogy, to illustrate his conviction that each man bears responsibility for the community of which he is part, and whose values he claims for himself. It is the same, though in a wider sense, as the Little Prince's responsibility for the rose which he claims as his own.

The corollary of responsibility towards others is humility in oneself. Not that one considers oneself of no value (for then there would be nothing to give), but that one is prepared to share oneself, to give oneself in the service of that unitary whole of which one is part:

3. Je comprends le sens de l'humilité. Elle n'est pas dénigrement de soi. Elle est le principe même de l'action. . . . Je puis agir sur ce dont je suis. Je suis part constituante de la communauté des hommes. (ibid., 213)

4. Sacrifice ne signifie ni amputation ni pénitence. Il est
   essentiellement un acte. Il est un don de soi-même à
   l'Etre dont on prétendra se réclamer.   (ibid., p. 231)

Once again, one detects a note of quasi-religious ardour. By
the act of sacrifice, an individual is able to transcend himself,
to ascend to the plane of Man, to leave the profane for the
sacred. This self-transcendance is not optional, but mandatory,
if men are properly to communicate with one another:

5. C'est par la voie du sacrifice gratuit que les hommes
   communiquent les uns avec les autres. Et par gratuit
   j'entends que la partie *utile* est inutile. Car l'idole qui
   reçoit les cadeaux et le sang et la vie devient *tous les*
   hommes.   (*Carnets*, p. 24)

The word *gratuit* here carries no connotation of worthless-
ness or gratuitousness. Rather it implies that the gift of oneself looks for no reward or recognition. It seeks no acclamation.
It happens in silence.

It follows that a suicide, or a stupid death resulting from
extravagant bravado, debase the concept of self-sacrifice as
Saint-Exupéry intends it; they spring from vanity.

6. Le sacrifice perd toute grandeur s'il n'est plus qu'une
   parodie ou un suicide.   (*Pilote de Guerre*, p. 93)

The concept of responsible sacrifice reiterates the theme of
fraternal collaboration and liberating ties already propounded
in *Vol de Nuit* and especially *Terre des Hommes*. As in these
two books, *Pilote de Guerre* emphasizes that by giving oneself,
one surpasses oneself and satisfies the spiritual need for
plénitude:

7. Le métier de témoin m'a toujours fait horreur. Que suis-
   je, si je ne participe pas? J'ai besoin, pour être, de participer. . . . D'être lié. De communier, De recevoir et de
   donner. D'être plus que moi-même. D'accéder à cette
   plénitude qui me gonfle si fort.   (ibid., pp. 183, 186)

E. Humanism

Christianity once provided the unifying moral force to which men could sacrifice their individuality and in which they could achieve spiritual communion with each other. Men were brothers in God:

> 1. L'homme était créé à l'image de Dieu. On respectait Dieu en l'homme. Les hommes étaient frères en Dieu. Ce reflet de Dieu conférait une dignité inaliénable à chaque homme. Les relations de l'homme avec Dieu fondaient avec évidence les devoirs de chacun vis-à-vis de soi-même ou d'autrui. (ibid., p. 222)

As Christianity no longer fills this need, it must be replaced. Men must be brothers *in* something, they must be united in the service *of* something. The last pages of *Pilote de Guerre* are an eloquent homage to Christianity, but to a Christianity in the past. God was the absolute depositary of all values which men strove to emulate – dignity, hope, brotherhood, charity. God's function as the 'One', 'l'idole dont nous sommes privés' (*Carnets*, p. 35), the ideal embodiment of these values, has passed, but the values remain; in the age of scientific enlightenment, Christianity is discredited, but the values which it taught are still alive:

> 2. si j'ai perdu le bénéfice de l'explication religieuse, il faut au moins que j'en transpose les valeurs, car elles sont nécessaires et fertiles. (*Carnets*, p. 40)

Thus, Saint-Exupéry does not exhort us to discard the religious inheritance out of hand, but to metamorphose it, to convert it in such a way that we are able to retain the benefits that accrue from its function as a civilizing agent.

And so, instead of worshipping God, we must worship *Man*, discernible through men. Each individual, insignificant in himself, is an ambassador of Man:

> 3. Ma civilisation repose sur le culte de l'Homme au travers des individus. (*Pilote de Guerre*, p. 219)

4. l'individu n'est qu'une route. L'Homme qui l'emprunte
compte seul. (ibid., p. 214)

Men need an ideal if their spiritual nature is to be nourished.
That ideal has been left to us in the legacy of Christianity; it
is the ideal of God *without* God. That is why, in his fervent
credo at the end of the book, Saint-Exupéry writes of civilization not as being founded on God, but inherited from God:

5. Ma civilisation, héritant de Dieu, a fait les hommes égaux
en l'Homme.
Ma civilisation, héritant de Dieu, a fait les hommes
frères en l'Homme. (ibid., pp. 224–225)

In short, Saint-Exupéry here wishes to discard Christianity,
while rescuing from the shipwreck the notion of an *ideal*, which
he can transform into his new religion, the religion of Man.
This ideal resumes in absolute terms all the virtues which his
work hitherto has declaimed: brotherhood, responsibility, self
abnegation:

6. Ma civilisation, héritière de Dieu, a fait chacun responsable de tous les hommes, et tous les hommes responsables
de chacun. Un individu doit se sacrifier au sauvetage d'une
collectivité, mais il ne s'agit point ici d'une arithmétique
imbécile. Il s'agit du respect de l'Homme au travers de
l'individu. La grandeur, en effet, de ma civilisation, c'est
que cent mineurs s'y doivent de risquer leur vie pour le
sauvetage d'un seul mineur enseveli. Ils sauvent l'Homme.
(ibid., p. 227)

This, one of the most eloquent passages in all Saint-Exupéry's
work, crystallizes the moral intention of both *Vol de Nuit* and
Terre des Hommes.

Saint-Exupéry goes on to explain how his Humanism
(which is spiritual) differs from the Humanism of the rational-
ists. Rational Humanism depends on words. The spiritual
Humanism here proposed is nothing if it is not expressed
through acts:

7. L'Humanisme s'est donné pour mission exclusive d'éclairer
et de perpétuer la primauté de l'Homme sur l'individu.

L'Humanisme a prêché l'Homme. Mais quand il s'agit de parler sur l'Homme, le langage devient incommode.
(ibid., p. 229)

8. L'Humanisme a négligé le rôle essential du sacrifice. Il a prétendu transporter l'Homme par les mots et non par les actes.   (ibid., p. 231)

It is essential that one should prove one's faith in Man by authentic acts of sacrifice to Man. One must suppress the individual for the greater glory of the Universal:

9. Je combattrai pour la primauté de l'Homme sur l'individu — comme de l'universel sur le particulier.
(ibid., p. 241)

The author rejects traditional Humanism because it is concerned with celebrating the existing, visible qualities of men. This he considers to be static and unproductive. One must go beyond this concept in favour of a militant, active Humanism which, by striving towards accomplishment, promises to reveal the submerged potential of Man. It is not a Humanism content with self-congratulation, but an idea demanding constant effort.

The distinction which Saint-Exupéry makes between *l'homme* (with a small *h*) and *l'Homme* (with a capital *H*), is most readily understood by his own image of the cathedral. The sum of individuals, he says, is no better than an ant-hill, but the spiritual value of Man which they represent is the foundation of Humanism. We must compare the individuals to stones, and the community to the cathedral which the stones together compose. Each one of the stones has meaning and purpose only in so far as it contributes to the edifice of which it is part. Thus, when we honour and respect individual men, we are honouring, through them, Man who is both in them and above them. The cathedral, in this analogy, may represent a small community (the pilots of *Vol de Nuit*, for example), or a civilization, but it is always the Universal that is expressed through the work of the community.

10. Car l'Homme de ma civilisation ne se définit pas à partir des hommes. Ce sont les hommes qui se définissent par lui. Il est en lui, comme en tout Etre, quelque chose que n'expliquent pas les matériaux qui le composent. Une cathédrale est bien autre chose qu'une somme de pierres. Elle est géométrie et architecture. Ce ne sont pas les pierres qui la définissent, c'est elle qui enrichit les pierres de sa propre signification. Ces pierres sont ennoblies d'être pierres d'une cathédrale.

(ibid., p. 220)

We are reminded of the *Lettre au Général X*: 'la vie de l'esprit commence là où un être "un" est conçu au-dessus des matériaux qui le composent'.

Men bound to each other in a community express, by the very act of submerging their individual identities in the community, the supreme value of Man – 'L'Homme commune mesure des camarades.'

Saint-Exupéry's Humanism is full of hope and poetry. He is not concerned with the man of kitchen-sink realism, only with the man of infinite possibilities of grandeur. His is a message of hope. He believes in the perfectibility of the human race, in the capacity of men to join together in fraternal ardour and avoid, in future, the petty quarrels which derive from their artificial divisions.

That the hope did not last is clear from events. Less than two years later, Saint-Exupéry wrote his *Lettre au Général X*, which was found among his belongings after his death, and published in *Le Figaro Littéraire*. We have already had cause to refer to it in the chapter on *Terre des Hommes*. It is a sad letter of disillusion and frustration, the letter of a man who despairs that he will ever be heard. 'J'ai l'impression de marcher vers les temps les plus noirs du monde,' he writes. What can I say to prevent it? *Que fait-il dire aux hommes?*

* * * * *

At the beginning of 1943, Saint-Exupéry published a very short book, less than 8,000 words in all, called *Lettre à Un Otage*.

As its title implies, it was addressed to a Frenchman still living in occupied France, namely the author's close friend Léon Werth. The book's purpose is to clarify the nature of the civilization they are together fighting to protect.

The author relates how, in 1940, he was in Lisbon on his way to the United States. There he observed a group of French emigrants, whose ties with everything that gave meaning to their lives were now severed, but who still played the game of living by profligate spending of their savings. It was all very absurd. The obscure quality of life was here missing.

What is that quality? What is it that makes the Sahara more alive than Lisbon? It is an essential value, a spiritual inheritance, which it is very difficult to describe in words, but which is revealed, sometimes, by a smile.

Saint-Exupéry recounts the story of his capture by the anarchists during the Spanish Civil War, of their difficulty in communication, and of his request for a cigarette. Then the 'miracle' happened, the soldier smiled, and the invisible thread which unites man with man was tightened. The smile is above language, above fanaticism; it is the expression of a profound respect for Man through men, a respect on which our civilization is based. Such is the respect which the emigrants in Lisbon have abandoned in their flight from material deprivation.

6

Le Petit Prince

Le Petit Prince was published in New York in 1943, only a few months after *Lettre à Un Otage*. It purports to be a story for children (and can be read as such), but the story illustrates the eternal truths which Saint-Exupéry had been at pains to convey in his other books, and which the 'grown-ups' who read them had been too stupid to understand.

In addressing his book to children, and making frequent, gently sarcastic remarks about the obscurantism of the adults, the author wishes to point out that his book has much to teach the 'grandes personnes', if only they would listen. Perhaps it is for the children to explain to them?

The author has crashed his aircraft in the desert. He is busy repairing it, when he is quite suddenly approached by a charming little prince with blond hair, who says to him, 'S'il vous plaît . . . dessine-moi un mouton . . .'

The author obliges, and friendship between the two unlikely castaways is established. The Little Prince tells how he is in love with a rose, on the planet where he lives, but her vanity and fickleness hurt him, so he decided to travel far from his planet. Before leaving, he was careful to collect all the seeds of the baobab trees, which threatened to spread all over the planet, and to sweep out his three volcanoes. Then he journeyed from one planet to another.

On one planet, he met a monarch without subjects, who enjoyed playing at being king, and was delighted to have the Little Prince as a temporary subject whom he could command. On another, there was the narcissist, whose only pleasure was to be admired. He, too, was alone on his planet, so his only admirer was himself. The third planet was the home of the drunkard, who was ashamed of being alcoholic, and drowned his shame in drink. The fourth planet sheltered the business-man, counting his money, making calculations, and claiming ownership of the stars. The final planet which the Little Prince visited was so small that day and night were each only a few minutes long. Here there lived a lamplighter, whose entire life was taken in lighting and putting out his lamp to keep time with the swift rotation of his planet. However absurd and frus-trating it may seem, the Little Prince felt respect for the lamp-lighter, because of all those he had visited, he was the only one who was looking after something other than himself.

Eventually, the Little Prince landed on earth, and was sur-prised to find it empty. He met a fox, who explained to him that the important thing in life is to 'tame' people, make friends with them, create ties with them, and then the world becomes orderly around them. 'On ne voit bien qu'avec le coeur,' says the fox, 'l'essentiel est invisible pour les yeux.'

You are forever responsible for the thing that you have tamed, says the fox. The Little Prince realizes that he is re-sponsible for his rose, left alone on his planet; once he has offered and accepted love, he has accepted responsibility.

Disappointed with earth, where the inhabitants turn in giddy circles and get nowhere because they have no sense of purpose or direction, the Little Prince leaves, as suddenly as he came, but not before telling the airman that his life may also hence-forth have a sense, because somewhere, in one of those stars, is a little prince who is his friend.

In *Terre des Hommes*, Saint-Exupéry had written,

> Mais la vérité, vous le savez, c'est ce qui simplifie le monde, et non ce qui crée le chaos. La vérité, c'est le langage qui dégage l'universal. (p. 134)

In *Le Petit Prince*, he set out to 'simplify the world'.

A. La Rose

The rose with which the prince is in love is a vain and capricious creature:

> 1. — Ah! je me réveille à peine . . . Je vous demande
>   pardon. . . . Je suis encore toute décoiffée . . .
>   Le Petit Prince, alors, ne put contenir son admiration:
>   — Que vous êtes belle!
>   — N'est-ce pas, répondit doucement la fleur. Je suis née
>   en même temps que le soleil.   (p. 31)

Her unreliability and contradictory nature causes him pain and heartache. He is too young to have learned the lesson that flowers are not to be heeded – they are to be cherished for their beauty alone:

> 2. il ne faut jamais écouter les fleurs. Il faut les regarder et
>   les respirer.   (p. 33)

It is obvious that the flower is symbolic of the feminine temperament which Saint-Exupéry never fully understood. It has been suggested that the prince's flower is, more precisely, a symbol of Consuelo, the author's wife. Their marriage had certainly been at once touchingly and childishly romantic, and at times tempestuous. Consuelo was, moreover, a striking beauty universally admired

Such can only be conjecture. Yet it is interesting to note how little Saint-Exupéry's bewilderment in the presence of women had changed over the years. The Little Prince's rose echoes very clearly the only other feminine character in his work, Geneviève in *Courrier Sud*:

> 3. Sans doute l'aimait-elle toujours, mais il ne faut pas trop
>   demander à une faible petite fille.
>   (*Courrier Sud*, p. 125)

It is instructive also to read the letters which Saint-Exupéry addressed to Renée de Saussine in his youth, in which the slightly hurt tone of one who does not comprehend the vagaries of the female heart is similar to that of the Little Prince:

4. C'est bien la première fois depuis Dakar que je puis vous parler sans amertume. Je vous en ai bien voulu! C'est curieux comme vous savez ne rien comprendre quand vous voulez.   (*Lettres de Jeunesse*, p. 141)

And yet, when the Little Prince has 'apprivoisé' his flower, he is prepared to sacrifice himself for her. Were he not to return to his planet, his rose would have no one to water her and protect her; she is so weak and naive, she would be helpless without him. She would wither and die. The prince accepts his responsibility for her; his duty is to 'seem to die' (*avoir l'air de mourir*) for her sake, in recognition of the bond which ties her to him.

B. Les Grandes Personnes

The grown-ups are short-sighted, mean, petty, selfish. They cannot understand anything intuitively, because they lack imagination, but must needs always have things explained. They have a veritable passion for facts and figures:

1. Les grandes personnes ne comprennent jamais rien toutes seules . . . elles ont toujours besoin d'explications.
                                        (p. 10)
2. Et les hommes manquent d'imagination. Ils répètent ce qu'on leur dit.   (p. 64)

The Little Prince's greatest pleasure is watching the sunset, which he can do as often as he likes on his small planet, simply by moving his chair a little. But grown-ups know no such pleasure. With their facts and figures, they are so busy taking themselves seriously, that they have no time for the simple beauties of life:

3. Je connais une planète où il y a un Monsieur cramoisi. Il n'a jamais respiré une fleur. Il n'a jamais regardé une étoile. Il n'a jamais aimé personne. Il n'a jamais rien fait d'autre que des additions. Et toute la journée il répète comme toi: 'Je suis un homme sérieux! Je suis un homme sérieux!' et ça le fait gonfler d'orgueil. Mais ce n'est pas un homme, c'est un champignon!   (p. 29)

The planets which the prince visits before his arrival on Earth are inhabited by men who each represent the follies and vices of mankind which Saint-Exupéry most regrets; the taste for power (the king), vanity (the narcissist), acquisitiveness (the businessman). They are all inward-looking, self-regarding, prisoners of their own imperious needs. Only the lamplighter leads a life devoted to something outside himself; his task, though apparently ludicrous, has a sense which theirs does not:

4. Celui-là, se dit le petit prince, tandis qu'il poursuivait plus loin son voyage, celui-là serait méprisé par tous les autres, par le roi, par le vaniteux, par le buveur, par le businessman. Cependant c'est le seul qui ne me paraisse pas ridicule. C'est, peut-être, parce qu'il s'occupe d'autre chose que de soi-même.   (p. 52)

Children intuitively understand the world in all its simplicity. Most men, when they cease to be children, forget the truths which they once knew with such clarity, and spend the rest of their lives contributing to chaos and confusion. They believe they know everything, as the sum of their 'knowledge' increases with age; but they have facts, not comprehension. Children do not need facts:

5. Mais, bien sûr, nous qui comprenons la vie, nous nous moquons bien des numéros!   (p. 20)

Saint-Exupéry, in *Le Petit Prince*, wants us to make a supreme effort to return to the essential truth of childhood. In that way, perhaps we may finally understand:

6. Piètre non-sens: les enfants qui ne comprennent point — c'est-à-dire seuls comprennent.   (*Carnets*, p. 133)

C. L'Apprivoisement

'Apprivoiser', says the fox, means 'to create bonds'. 'Si tu m'apprivoises, nous aurons besoin l'un de l'autre . . . ma vie sera comme ensoleillée.' The fox asks the Little Prince to tame him, so that they might be bound to each other by mutual need. Only then will their solitude cease:

1. On ne connaît que les choses que l'on apprivoise, dit le renard. Les hommes n'ont plus le temps de rien connaître. Ils achètent des choses toutes faites chez les marchands. Mais comme il n'existe point de marchands d'amis, les hommes n'ont plus d'amis. Si tu veux un ami, apprivoise-moi!   (p. 69)

Just as the pilots of the Line, united in mutual need, are responsible for each other, so the Little Prince will be responsible for the fox, as he is already for his rose. Disinterested love carries the heaviest responsibility:

2. Les hommes ont oublié cette vérité, dit le renard. Mais tu ne dois pas l'oublier. Tu deviens responsable pour toujours de ce que tu as apprivoisé. Tu es responsable de ta rose. . . .   (p. 74)

The fox shares with the Little Prince his own secret of life. It is a very simple secret, as all truth is simple, but it is important because men have lost sight of it. It is a secret which Saint-Exupéry tried to impart, in more high-blown language, in *Pilote de Guerre*. It is this:

3. Voici mon secret. Il est très simple: on ne voit bien qu'avec le coeur. L'essentiel est invisible pour les yeux. (p. 72)

Is this not identical with the message of *Pilote de Guerre*, that the intelligence is incapable of perceiving reality, which is revealed only to one who sees with the spirit? Substitute *Esprit* for *coeur*, and *intelligence* for *yeux* in the above passage, and the lesson is the same.

What Saint-Exupéry is saying is this: childhood has much to teach manhood, because a child has the gift of spontaneous, intuitive understanding of what matters in the world. The child tells us that we must learn to penetrate appearances in order to discover hidden realities which the intelligence, with its analytic methods, is incapable of perceiving. The child is closer to poetic truth than we; with divine and simple grace, and without any fuss, the child understands the world through love:

4. L'intelligence ne vaut qu'au service de l'amour.
(*Pilote de Guerre*, p. 205)

Surprisingly, this graceful and blazingly simple book has been subjected to the most diverse interpretations. Some critics, impervious to its message, have set their intellectual faculties to work in an effort to analyse it out of existence, and are thus guilty of an unconscious irony which, one suspects, would have greatly amused its author. Renée Zeller, for example, considers the two active volcanoes on the prince's planet to be symbolic of Charity and Hope, while the extinct volcano, which the prince none the less still tends, symbolizes Saint-Exupéry's lost religious faith! For Yves Le Hir, the disabled aircraft which the narrator is trying to put in order when the Little Prince first appears, is a symbol of the author's soul. R.-M. Albérès, whose whole thesis looks like an attempt to establish the author's impotence, suggests that the Little Prince is 'the child that Saint-Exupéry never had'. While Pierre de Boisdeffre is simply dismissive. The book, he says, excites teachers, but bores children to death ('enthousiasme les instituteurs et assomme les enfants'). Rumbold and Stewart see the book as a satire on those aspects of American life which Saint-Exupéry found most distasteful.

Jean-Claude Ibert comes closest to an understanding of the author's intention. He says that Saint-Exupéry was enchanted by the child's capacity to see things with an interior, subjective vision, and by his unshakeable confidence that what he saw was indeed so. A child cannot be deterred by argument, for truth, as he sees it, has nothing to do with reason:

> Ce qui l'enchantait, chez les enfants, c'est surtout leur adhésion totale à leurs croyances, leur singulière aptitude à situer le possible au coeur même de ce qui paraît être impossible, et leur merveilleuse disponibilité affective qui leur permet de donner de l'âme à ce qui est, par définition, inanimable. Il décelait en eux, à l'état naturel, cet élan d'amour incontrôlé qui doit conduire les hommes à s'accomplir dans une quête de pureté où se trouvent exprimés à la fois la valeur de leur condition et le sens de

leur universalité. Les enfants ont des choses une vision
intérieure, subjective: ils les *apprivoisent*. Saint-Exupéry
s'est efforcé de nous montrer comment nous pouvions
adopter leur *point de vue*.

(*Saint-Exupéry*, by J.-C. Ibert, p. 89)

And, as if to help us see matters from a child's point of view,
he illustrated the book himself with the drawings of a child.

One thing is sure: there is a large element of autobiography
in *Le Petit Prince*. Both Saint-Exupéry and his creation felt
isolated and at loggerheads with a world which would not see
the truth. Saint-Exupéry, who retained the charm of infancy
well into his manhood, was never at ease 'on earth'. His imagination took flights of fancy which lifted him into the world of
make-believe and left his friends far behind. He would have
been happy, one suspects, on the Little Prince's planet, shifting
his chair to watch the sunset.

7

Citadelle

As early as 1939, Saint-Exupéry had begun writing the book which he intended to be his major literary achievement – *Citadelle*. 'Next to this,' he told Pierre Dalloz, 'all my other books are mere exercises.' It was to be the book which resumed a lifetime's thought and experience, the summit to which his previous work had been striving. 'Que faut-il dire aux hommes?' he had asked, in near despair, in the *Lettre au Général X. Citadelle* was the answer.

He worked on the book during the last year of his life with feverish intensity. He said that it would take him another ten years to complete, but the zeal with which he now approached the task indicated that he had something like a premonition that time was against him. He often referred to *Citadelle* as his posthumous work. A letter quoted by Pierre Chevrier shows that, even in 1942, two years before he died and some months before the publication of *Le Petit Prince*, his writing of *Citadelle* was an obsession:

> Ça paraîtra à ma mort, car je n'aurai jamais fini. J'ai sept cents pages. Si je les travaillais comme un simple article, ces sept cents pages de gangue, il me faudrait déjà dix ans, rien que de mise au point. Je les travaillerai simplement jusqu'au bout de mes forces. Je ne ferai plus rien d'autre au monde. Je n'ai plus aucun sens par moi-même. Je me sens menacé, vulnérable, limité dans le temps, je veux finir mon arbre. Guillaumet est mort. Je veux vite finir mon arbre. Je veux vite devenir autre chose que moi. . . . Je crois que ça tient maintenant à moi comme une ancre de fond.

Embittered by the ideological chaos of his time, and the fratricidal quarrels which he had been forced to witness, Saint-

Exupéry wanted to set forth his ideas in a form utterly devoid of contemporary application. They must be above and beyond mere polemics. So he placed his citadel in the desert, where the absence of all tangible riches affords the peace in which men may learn.

Of course, he was right. The book was never finished. In addition to the huge manuscript, large passages had been dictated into a dictaphone. We know what a perfectionist Saint-Exupéry was in his writing; the final draft of *Vol de Nuit* was a mere quarter the size of the original. He would sometimes write scores of versions of the same page before deciding which was the best. It is therefore certain that he would not have published *Citadelle* in the form that we know it. It would have been pared down, re-organized, polished, sharpened. As it stands, it is rambling, disorderly, repetitive, often obscure. But it is none the less the passionately eloquent testament of a man who wanted desperately to be heard.

A. The Meaning

In *Lettre à un Otage*, Saint-Exupéry had written: 'une politique n'a de sens qu'à condition d'être au service d'une évidence spirituelle.' (p. 62) *Pilote de Guerre* had confirmed his conviction that men were capable of attaining a spiritual unity above the political or religious differences which beset them. In writing *Citadelle*, he wanted to show men *how*; he wanted to show that a theory of government in which authority rested on a mystical foundation was at least conceivable.

Saint-Exupéry wants to re-awaken the religious/mystical element in men by offering them a new myth which might be powerful enough to inflame their hearts. That new myth is a Mystique of Man, conceived as the symbol of human perfectibility, and incarnated in the Leader. *Citadelle* is the Bible of Man, dedicated to the adoration of that universal man which is in all men, and which can be released by the vocational life, by sacrifice, by love: 'Citadelle, je te construirai dans le coeur de l'homme.' (p. 516)

The possible perfectibility of man is the ideal which has replaced the established perfection of God.

One must approach *Citadelle* with the reverence due to a new Bible, a new Revelation. One must read it as a long, didactic poem. Only then may the reader hear the voice of this extraordinary book, be swept along in the wake of its extravagant tone.

B. The Subject

A desert chieftain, about to inherit absolute power from his father, is instructed by the latter on the government of men. He listens and learns. Once he has himself become supreme master of the empire, he observes what forces exalt his people, and what debases them. He thereby reaches conclusions as to what strengthens the empire, and what weakens it. That, in rounded terms, is the subject of *Citadelle*.

The theme is presented in a disconnected series of meditations and parables, which owe their unity to the Biblical tone and to the continuous presence of the chieftain. These meditations are the consummation of all the themes in the Saint-Exupéry corpus from *Courrier Sud* onwards.

The permanence of the 'domaine', says the chieftain, is constantly threatened by a variety of forces, both internal and external. The external forces are the more dangerous: the temptation offered by adultery, false prophets, misdirected pity, the stupidity of generals, the destructive power of logical intelligence, the inertia of sedentary life, the evil of possessive love, the insidious influence of those who *do* nothing.

The chieftain's purpose is not to guarantee the happiness of his people by offering them material comfort, which is a deceptive good, rotting the soul and bringing ultimate misery. His purpose is rather to encourage their spiritual self-transcendance. To this end, he must reveal to them the meaning of the 'domaine', the significance of the empire, by means of ceremony and rite, and the establishment of a hierarchy. His people are then encouraged to ascend, to become, to enrich themselves by sacrifice, by giving themselves in exchange for their work. Their ultimate aim is to achieve the Absolute, the Ideal, which is Man (or, to use another name, God).

C. The Leader

    1. je forge l'homme.   (p. 513)

The chieftain's duty is to create the Absolute towards which he wishes his subjects to strive. He creates a mystique of Man. He must himself be the incarnation of that mystique, the symbol of human perfectibility, if the people are to have a *visible* ideal that they may emulate. In respecting the Chief, they acknowledge the possibility that is within them. He is the symbol of their faith, the living embodiment of their ideal. They must therefore not only have confidence in him, but love him, believe in him, accept him as *nécessité naturelle*, as the expression of qualities they wish to release in themselves. A reflection in the *Carnets* serves to illustrate the mystical function of the Chief:

    2. La divinité s'exprime à travers l'individu qui va contre le
       goût moyen.   (*Carnets*, p. 204)

It is necessary that the Chief be a hard man, since he must impose his will on his subjects, force them to become themselves *in spite of* themselves, without their necessarily understanding why or how. He must oblige them to follow paths which will lead to their own fulfilment, and to the flowering of the civilization of which they are part.

In this respect, it is clear that the Chief is a grander realization of Rivière in *Vol de Nuit*, Rivière who also held absolute power over his pilots, and to whom they owed unquestioning allegiance. Rivière's concept of action was a mystical one, in which he himself had unshakeable faith. He demanded that his pilots should share that faith, for the community which he had founded would only be justified if the pilots were ready to sacrifice themselves for it.

Like a medieval monarch, the Chief holds absolute power by divine-right. His subjects must accept him as *nécessité naturelle*, as a legislator who knows better than they how to make them live in peace and self-fulfilment. They must be prepared and happy to submit to his infallible will, however arbitrary it may appear. The arbitrariness of his power is essential if he is to create a society in which his subjects may realize themselves, and especially eradicate the evil which besieges their soul and which, without him, would drag them into mediocrity.

Is the Chief then a despot? Perhaps Saint-Exupéry wants him to be a benevolent despot, since he does endow him with qualities of moderation and love as well as omnipotence. He sometimes appears to be a strong but compassionate *pater-familias* rather than an unscrupulous tyrant. And yet the author (if he is proposing the society of *Citadelle* as a realizable model and not just an imaginary Utopia) gives us no indication as to how we are to be *sure* of the Chief's compassion. As he himself wrote, the idea of a benevolent despot is a myth, since if he is a despot, he is not elected, and if he is not elected, how are we to be certain of his benevolence?

> 3. 'Le bon tyran'; ce n'est qu'un mythe, car rien ne nous fait prévoir un mode de sélection qui le crée nécessairement bon.   (*Carnets*, p. 60)

Good he must be, as he is the sole depositary of justice. His justice has a breadth of vision which ordinary mortals are not required to comprehend, but simply to respect.

Most important of all (and this concept alone softens the otherwise brutal tone of the Chief's authority), he is the servant of his people. He is more in subjection to his subjects than any of them are to him. The author insists that there is no question of the Chieftain's *enslavement* of his people; on the contrary, he is their *messenger*:

> 4. Et je n'ai point fait un dieu de l'empire afin qu'il asservît les hommes. Je ne sacrifie point les hommes à l'empire.

Mais je fonde l'empire pour en remplir les hommes et les
en animer, et l'homme compte plus pour moi que l'empire.
C'est pour fonder les hommes que je les ai soumis à
l'empire. Ce n'est point pour fonder l'empire que j'ai
asservi les hommes. Mais abandonne donc ce langage qui
ne mène à rien et distingue la cause de l'effet et le maître
du serviteur. Car il n'est que relation et structure et
dépendance interne. Moi qui règne, je suis plus soumis à
mon peuple qu'aucun de mes sujets ne l'est à moi. Moi
qui monte sur ma terrasse et reçois leurs plaintes nocturnes
et leurs balbutiements et leurs cris de souffrance et le
tumulte de leurs joies pour en faire un cantique à Dieu,
je me conduis donc pour leur serviteur. C'est moi le
messager qui les rassemble et les emporte. C'est moi
l'esclave chargé de leur litière. C'est moi leur traducteur.

(Citadelle, p. 633)

A cardinal element of this idea is the notion that a Chief
needs his people as much as they need him. Thus the relationship of ruler to ruled is an expression of their mutual necessity.
It is the ultimate *bond* of which all the previous writing of
Saint-Exupéry was a celebration:

5. Nous chercher un chef, c'est, pour nous, nous chercher
   nous-mêmes. Un chef c'est celui qui a infiniment besoin
   des autres. Et nous voulons qu'on ait besoin de nous . . .
   Un chef, c'est celui qui nous *attire* au lieu d'acheter comme
   un octroi de faveurs l'acceptation de notre aide.

(Carnets, p. 23)

In other words, human nature needs leadership to crystallize
and shape its obscure urges to self-fulfilment, and rescue it
from the temptations of mediocrity.

D. God

1. Car Tu es, Seigneur, la commune mesure.   (p. 993)

With these final words of *Citadelle*, Saint-Exupéry suggests
that God is the supreme unifying force to which the spirituality
of man aspires.

We may reasonably pause here and admit confusion. Has it

not already been established that the idea of the perfectibility
of man is the Absolute Ideal which men must strive to attain?
If this be so (and all Saint-Exupéry's writing leaves no doubt
that it is), then why the need for God? Is He an alternative,
an addition, or a symbol of the same idea expressed in a different way?

We know, on Saint-Exupéry's own admission, and on the
evidence of his writing, that he did not accept the belief in God
as valid. Why, then, raise the matter now?

God is mentioned on almost every page of *Citadelle*. But
what sort of Deity remains vague and imprecise. The concept
is wide open to disparate interpretations, and even within the
pages of *Citadelle* it is bafflingly inconsistent. Only one thing
is certain: it is not the God of orthodox Christianity.

Most commentators are agreed that the God of *Citadelle*
approaches most closely the God of the Deists. He is a kind
of Bergsonian 'élan vital'[1] (Rumbold and Stewart), 'un Dieu
qui ne s'incarne point,' (Pierre de Boisdeffre), 'aspiration déiste
qui crée elle-même son objet d'adoration' (Luc Estang). How
far this concept is removed from the Christian God is clear
from several passages in which His inaccessibility is averred.
He does not listen to, nor does He respond to, prayer, a fact
which in no way invalidates the point of praying:

> 2. Car je n'avais point touché Dieu, mais un dieu qui se
> laisse toucher n'est plus un dieu. Ni s'il obéit à la prière.
> Et pour la première fois, je devinais que la grandeur de la
> prière réside d'abord en ce qu'il n'y est point répondu et
> que n'entre point dans cet échange la laideur d'un com-
> merce. Et que l'apprentissage de la prière est l'apprentis-
> sage du silence. Et que commence l'amour là seulement
> où il n'est plus de don à attendre. L'amour d'abord est
> exercise de la prière et la prière exercice du silence.
>
> (pp. 684–5)

[1] Henri Bergson (1859–1941), philosopher, in his *Evolution Créatrice*
(1907) rejected the Darwinian thesis of random mutation in evolution, and
proposed the idea of an original impulse in life, which he called *L'élan vital*,
and which added the psychological factor in evolution, being a common
effort on the part of individual organisms to create new species.

One cannot help thinking that, had Saint-Exupéry lived to edit his manuscript, he would have expurgated a great deal of what is nebulous, and clarified the inconsistencies. It is unjust, in the circumstances, to charge him with woolly-mindedness, as some have done.

For the real answer one has to refer to earlier writings, and then apply them, with caution, to *Citadelle*. Saint-Exupéry always regretted the loss of religious faith, and with it the rigorous moral constraint which it imposed. As we have seen, he believed that constraint was a liberating influence, and that men needed to climb towards an ideal:

> 3. La contrainte morale ne nous gêne point, nous l'appelons de tous nos voeux, nous savons bien qu'il faut de dures lois pour pétrir des êtres forts. Cela nous aiderait pour nous y soumettre que l'on inventât un Dieu. Non tant à cause des récompenses promises — car la première, la seule qui pour nous compte est de grandir — mais pour donner avec amour, pour encenser de nos sacrifices nécessaires l'idole dont nous sommes privés. Trop tôt sevrés de Dieu à l'âge où l'on se réfugie encore, voici qu'il nous faut lutter pour la vie en petits bonhommes solitaires.
>
> (*Carnets*, p. 35)

It would be a help if we were to invent a God, to replace the idol of which we have been too soon deprived! In *Vol de Nuit*, the author had spoken of religious rites which may seem absurd, but which mould men (p. 18).

We are now approaching the kernel. What Saint-Exupéry has in fact done in *Citadelle* is to re-invent God. Knowing that men cannot aspire to the ideal of Man without, frequently, an artificial stimulus, he has introduced a spur. God is a creation of man for his own ends.

God has been invented by man as a symbol of his own self-transcendence. God is the name given by Saint-Exupéry to his central idea of man's possible ascension from materialism to spirituality. Put in another way, God is the *promise* of a postulated world in which spirituality will be finally triumphant over materialism (André Devaux).

In conceiving his ideal society in *Citadelle*, Saint-Exupéry, aware that man was wretched without God, decided to invent Him as the summit of his pyramid. In the same way that man must 'become' himself in order to discover himself, so God must be invented in order to be discovered.

Thus, God is not a Supreme Being. Nor is he the Ideal. That Ideal is Man. God is not a static concept at all. He is the *process of ascension* towards the Ideal. He is the stimulus, the spur which men need to create Man.

God is necessary to convey the spirituality of man's struggle to elevate himself. It matters little that He is invented. He remains true, in the sense that He is an integral part in the scale of values likewise invented by man. Man creates God, and then worships his own creation.

E. Opinions

There are critics who regard *Citadelle* as the crowning masterpiece of Saint-Exupéry's work (Pierre Chevrier, Georges Pellissier), others who consider it the tired output of a disillusioned man, 'les songeries d'un héros déçu'. (André Beucler)

Whatever their opinions as to the merit of the book, critics are divided on the significance of the Chieftain. Many have been repelled by the principle of one man in absolute authority forcing others against their will to do his bidding, whether or no it be (in his view) for their own good. There is the world of difference between proposing a moral lesson, which the individual should then apply to himself, and imposing the lesson without the individual's consent, or even his comprehension. No doubt Saint-Exupéry understood the nuances of his message, but they are not always clear to the reader. Coming so soon after the war, with the bitter memory of Hitler still fresh, it is no wonder that many cried, with *Time* magazine, 'Fascist'.

Every reader has noticed the undeniable Nietzschean influence which pervades *Citadelle*. I cannot resist quoting from one particularly florid denunciation of the work: